VOLUNTEER LEADERSHIP

7 DISCIPLINES to UNDISPUTED SUCCESS

VOLUNTEER LEADERSHIP

7 DISCIPLINES to UNDISPUTED SUCCESS

What Every Volunteer Leader Needs To
Overcome Barriers and Help Others Succeed

David A. Kitchen   **Michael B. Lattimore**

ML

MARILEE Publishing
Altadena, CA

ML

MARILEE Publishing

Volunteer Leadership: 7 Disciplines to Undisputed Success
Copyright © 2018 by David Kitchen, Michael Lattimore.

MARILEE Publishing
PO Box 238, Altadena, CA 91003-0238
www.marileepublishing.com

ISBN-13: 978-1732248205 (Paperback)
ISBN-10: 1732248206

Library of Congress Control Number 2018952026

Editor: Brad Jorgenson
Production: Marilee Publishing

Printed in the U.S.A.
First Printing, 2018

Ordering Information: Special discounts are available for volume purchases by schools, corporations, associations, and others. To place an order, call (562) 548-2284 or contact publisher at the address above.

This book reflects the authors' present recollections of observations and personal experiences over time. Some names and characteristics have been changed to protect the innocent or guilty, and some dialogue and events have been compressed. Both the publisher and author(s) regret any unintentional harm resulting from the book.

First Edition

DEDICATION

To our mom, Marilyn, who taught us to stand up for what we believe and to keep it real. To our brother, Lee, who always stood in his truth and protected those who couldn't protect themselves. You both helped us become the leaders we are today, and will always be with us in spirit!

TABLE OF CONTENTS

*"Don't let someone else's opinion
of you become your reality."*

– Motivational Speaker Les Brown

FOREWORD

As the elder brother of David A. Kitchen, I have always been a scientist at heart. Ever since David was a wee lad, I enjoyed conducting experiments. I had been warned by my mother that the sweet chocolate "medicine" known as Ex-Lax was not to be consumed extravagantly. She warned me there would be dire consequences from eating too much. This I could not believe and conducted an experiment with the help of my very willing and curious subject. Guess who? It was so sweet to the taste! I think David liked the taste, but not the end result.

Being a young scientist in the making, I knew I required an experiment to fully test this theory. My grandmother had already described me quite accurately when she exclaimed one day, "Boy, you don't believe that fat meat is greasy!"

I'd like you to understand that David has always had the dynamic leadership qualities of Courage, Willingness and Determination to see things through to the end. Not even the unpleasant aftermath of being my Ex-Lax guinea pig could weaken his trust.

When I look back on that event, I realize that as leaders we don't always fully know what the outcome will be. Often there will be unexpected results from our volunteer leadership experience. Some of these results will afford us an opportunity to release old beliefs about ourselves as leaders, other people, and even service itself.

Some of these beliefs may be old ideas that we have been clinging to for many years and it can be extremely unsettling to have our belief systems shaken to the core.

The experience of volunteer leadership can also be very purifying. It can afford us the opportunity to learn new ideas and methods of effective Servant Leadership, releasing the "old" beliefs and ideas.

In "Volunteer Leadership" David teaches us how to be flexible leaders and to "look for the pony"[1] in the mounds of seemingly "garbage" that can appear in the leader's learning landscape.

In spring 2017, the number of people in the United States who had conducted volunteer work within the last 12 months amounted to 67.81 million. Samantha Jo Warfield, a Spokeswoman for CNCS (Corporation for National and Community Service), the federal agency with a primary focus on fostering volunteerism, had this to say back in 2014:

"Volunteering is a core American value. Our research has found that a large numbers of Americans — more than 1 in 4 — regularly volunteer in their communities, and this rate has stayed relatively stable over the past 12 years."

Today, many nonprofit agencies report that they are experiencing a downward trend in volunteer numbers. David's personal experience reveals that many volunteers, especially volunteer leaders, experience the downside of volunteerism and are turned off. They complain of burnout, overwork, pessimism, and an overall "bad taste in the mouth" from their service experience. Why is this?

In this book, David offers a special insider's look at the treasures he has mined from his many years of servant leadership in Toastmasters International and as a corporate trainer. He has also applied his extraordinary interpersonal and intrapersonal gifts in service to forging answers to questions such as these:

"How do I navigate the road of volunteer leadership and emerge unscathed by the seemingly negative aspects of human behavior encountered along the way?"

"How do I transmute poison into medicine so that the disappointments and frustrations of leadership do not turn me away from my calling to be a servant leader?"

David explores these ideas and offers solutions in the form of veritable principles from his lifelong experience as a volunteer leader. He is a giver, a servant leader with an unshakeable belief in humanity and one who has always been, at heart, a peacemaker and mediator. In Volunteer Leadership he speaks his word of experience with tips and insights that promise to make your road of servant leadership a little less bumpy and perhaps even more forgiving for yourself and others. He reminds us that not all that looks like candy is candy.

> [1] *A young boy, deemed a perpetual optimist, saw a wagon load of manure dumped in the street when the wagon cart broke down. He immediately pounced on the top of the mound and started digging as he exclaimed, "There has GOT to be a PONY in here somewhere!"*

Reverend Michael B. Lattimore, M.A.
August 2, 2018

"You can have everything in life you want, if you will just help other people get what they want"

- Motivational Speaker Zig Ziglar

PREFACE

A "Volunteer" is someone who freely offers to take part in a task or project with no financial gain. In turn, a "Volunteer Leader" leads a group of volunteers and/or facilitates feedback within an organization to help improve volunteer support and recruitment, and/or inspire volunteers to make a difference. There are plenty of reasons why people serve as volunteers or volunteer leaders. For some, it may be to give back or make a difference in someone's life. For others, it may create an opportunity to discover new knowledge or learn a new skill. Whatever the reason, there are a couple of common threads: 1) We help others and we grow, and 2) We help others and others help us. We grow by serving as a volunteer leader through the philosophy we know today as "Servant Leadership." It enriches lives and is the fabric of what builds better relationships.

Acquiring the benefits of Servant Leadership takes great discipline. Discipline leads to greater flexibility and control over our lives. Through discipline we become effective leaders. Through discipline and service to others, every volunteer can become a great leader and achieve undisputed success.

So, what is "Undisputed Success?" Simply put, it's success that is not doubted, challenged or disputed. Let's say your goal is to persuade five volunteers to feed the hungry on skid row. If you find five people to join you, without a doubt, you have successfully achieved your goal. It is undisputed. Boxing fighters, undefeated in their weight class, are classified as "undisputed champions."

The term "success" may be a matter of perspective. What is success to one person may not be success to another. But, there are some qualities that all people would consider as conditions for attaining success, irrespective of experience or belief. These would be social and behavioral qualities that inspire society.

There is a volume of social and behavioral qualities, as well as opportunities, that lead to attaining undisputed success. An employee effecting policy change in the workplace by speaking up for equality and fairness is an example of a good social quality. Tutoring a fellow classmate through a tough school subject matter to attain a successful grade would demonstrate a wonderful behavioral quality. Helping others to realize their potential or accomplish their goals can be a true measure of undisputed success. This is the hallmark of why volunteers serve as leaders.

Becoming a better leader depends upon helping others to discover their leadership power. Some people may be unable to see themselves in a leadership position. The book shares insider observations of how ordinary situations could lead a volunteer to learning how to lead in a volunteer organization. It reveals a side of leadership that some volunteer leaders won't share, in fear that if people learn the truth, volunteers would run for the hills!

Discipline is an important aspect of both truth and undisputed success. It is how volunteers walk the talk. Only through discipline can volunteer leaders serve as trusted 'truth tellers" to help others uncover their leadership power. Discipline can help shift the behavior of self-serving leaders to actual servant leaders.

Leading in an organization can provide a solid foundation for helping each of us become the type of person we desire to be. What volunteer leaders do today carves the path to what our world can become in the future. All that we are is based on the many people who have helped us along the way. The universe creates this wonderful opportunity; when we help others, they will help us. It is the law of reciprocity. When we give, others give. When we give, the universe gives. When we help, the universe helps us. Everything a volunteer leader ever needs can be attained when he or she reaches out to help another human being.

The hidden gift is that we uncover and discover who we are. When we practice discipline to do this, success begins to show up in our lives!

Some may argue against this premise. But those who serve as volunteer leaders won't dispute this: any success we want can be achieved by simply helping others succeed!

"The best way to find yourself is to lose yourself in the service of others"

- Mahatma Ghandi

INTRODUCTION

Leadership is a road less traveled. The purpose of this book is to encourage any volunteer to step up as a volunteer leader to make a difference in the world. Leadership is the foundation for learning to stretch your skills and talents and accomplishing your life goals. Striving for stretch goals is like having an itch that is hard to reach and scratch. But when you reach it, oh what a feeling! It's euphoric.

Can you remember your first experience that led you to KNOW you were meant to lead? I do. I wrote a passage about it called *How I Learned to Build a Bridge*, located in the Appendix section. The chapters and content in this book share lessons learned from vast, recollected experiences in volunteer leadership. It shares insights about volunteer leadership for existing and aspiring volunteer leaders. It takes an inside look into behaviors leaders often discover after their decision to say "yes" to leading as a volunteer. The stories share personal perspectives of seven disciplines on how to find undisputed success through helping others step into their purpose; to be the leader God intended you to be.

The origin of the word discipline comes from the *discipulis*, the Latin word for pupil; which also links to the word *disciple* (a follower of Jesus Christ in his lifetime). Every leader can benefit from genuine discipline, support, and guidance. Many of us rely on our higher power, who for many of us is God. Some readers might have a difference of opinion about the reference to God. If it helps, think of the word GOD as an acronym for "Good Orderly Direction!" Additionally, various people will have different views on leadership. Some people will read this book and say "ah, that stuff won't work" or "this is a bunch of hogwash." Others will read it and think "Wow, this was very insightful." Either way, it's a perception of individual reality. That is how serving in a leadership role works. As a leader, everyone is not going to agree with you. Everyone may not see your vision. Some will think your leadership style is great. Others may think your leadership style sucks! It doesn't matter. It's your journey. What matters most is your contribution and commitment to that journey.

Learning how to be successful volunteer leader begins with understanding your reason for wanting to lead. It could be to network and make connections with others. Or it may be to learn new or enhanced team-building skills. Some people serve to give back to others because someone helped them. Whatever your reason, it can create extraordinary opportunities in your life and help you to discover your life's purpose.

Volunteering can keep our skills relevant and help us stay youthful in spirit. It has led to one curiosity; can volunteering actually keep you feeling young? Experts in the health and wellness field believe so. This would be a good reason to serve as a volunteer leader.

CEO of PlayMore Corporate Wellbeing Rona Lewis, a volunteer leader, publishes a blog at www.PlayMoreCW.com to educate people on how volunteering affects everyone for the better. Lewis advocates:

"What is volunteering, really? Overall, it's kindness with a commitment. Volunteering can develop skills that will help

*further careers and improve growth and development.
Volunteering can make you healthier. Being kind produces
a hormone called oxytocin, which helps keep our hearts
healthy by relaxing the cells along the walls of our arteries.
This allows better blood flow to the heart and other organs,
thereby reducing blood pressure and risk of heart disease. It
might even lead to a longer life. One global study found
that people who volunteer have better overall health
outcomes than those who don't, leading to a 22* percent
lower mortality rate *after researchers followed up with
study groups years later. Who knew being kind could be so
healthy? Give it a shot, you may live a little longer…"*

That is incredible insight. Can you believe it? Experts believe
that volunteering can provide mental, physical, and spiritual
stimulation. But, come on, volunteering helping us live
longer? What?!? Actually, this was a question posed in a
2013 Media Spotlight article written for the Psychology
Today magazine. Taken from a case study, researchers at
Stony Brook and Arizona State University studied the effects
of volunteering and mortality across different subsamples.
Through direct and statistical analysis; as well as relationship
testing related to medical histories, age and other
considerations; this study too purported that "volunteering"
appeared to reduce risk of death by 25 percent."

If that is the case, let's get busy volunteering!

"People want to be on a team . . . to be part of something bigger than themselves . . . to be in a situation where they feel they are doing something for the greater good."

— 5-Time NCAA Winning Basketball Coach Mike Krzyzewski

DISCIPLINE #1

EVERYONE LOVES A WINNER, SO BE ONE

Let's get right to the point. Leading is not always the easiest thing to do. It requires steady discipline and the ability to seek understanding rather than being understood. Sometimes team leaders are the first to learn of a team issue, sometimes they are the last ones to find out. Volunteer leaders are charged with responsibility for their own actions, as well as the actions of others. Great leaders give credit to their teams when all goes well, and take the blame when things go wrong. This shows appreciation and love for your team. Volunteers want to be appreciated.

By human instinct, everyone wants to be a part of a winning and successful team. Ever witness a team that accomplished a seemingly hopeless goal? How many times have you heard a person express, "I was on that team!" OR "I helped make that happen!" We put it on our resumes. We tell our friends and family about it. Heck, we tell anyone who listens! The truth is people want to succeed and want their leader to succeed. When we were kids in Chicago playing on the railroad tracks, (who didn't do that in the Midwest?) we knew: when you see that train coming, get out of the way!

1

Yeah, we felt some of our fair-weather comrades would want nothing more than to see one of us get smacked by the train. But, when any of us leaped over the track to escape from being hit by that barreling train, EVERYONE celebrated.

The same is true with successfully leading in a volunteer organization. Everyone celebrates when team members succeed in accomplishing a goal, even those who may not have agreed with the team mission. There are times volunteer leaders may feel people want to see them fail. There are articles, social media posts, and books on why people want others to fail: jealousy, envy, spitefulness, despise, and the list goes on. Is this necessarily true?

When we were kids, we played with others who did not like us for whatever reasons, even when we played on those railroad tracks. But, so what! We were all doing the same thing. We got a rush seeing others escape from being smacked by a train. And in doing so we saw ourselves as winners. We surrounded ourselves with other kids who were daredevils and disciplined enough to keep from being hit by a train. Everyone wanted to be a winner.

Now, hold on! This is not an endorsement for anyone to play on the train tracks. The point is this: Get out of the way of the negative people wanting you to fail! Surround yourself, instead, with the people who want you to succeed! Practice being the winner your team members want you to be.

Look at this in a positive light. As a colleague and a good friend Joan would say, "...when we step up as a leader, seems like someone always wants to take our head off!" Of course, that is just a figure of speech. Let's face it, as volunteer leaders we do feel that way. Don't call it paranoia though. Some people ARE out to get you!

Understand that some people are carrying around their unhealed early family experiences. They may have had to struggle for position and recognition in their families when they were younger. There is a good chance that this competitiveness will show up when they join your team. Don't take it personal. It's not about you. It's only their emotional trigger showing up and driving them to react from a memory of old hurt. When leading a team, knowing this up front will help avoid the pitfalls of feeling hurt, or as some disgruntled people would say, "pissed off." Avoid taking things personally. In the long run, there is no point in spending your valuable time character assassinating your detractors. Team members often want to emulate the behavior they see in their leader. Members are proud to follow a leader who demonstrates charisma, respect, courage, and loyalty to the team and its goals. It takes discipline to practice to be the type of volunteer leader who can lead their team to undisputed success!

Here are three (3) positive perspectives to help enhance awareness, demonstrate courage, leadership faith and avoid potential setbacks:

Embrace Resistance

During every leadership journey, volunteer leaders will face resistance. If managed well, resistance can catapult your team to reach greater success. The greater the resistance, the greater the success. Ever flown a kite on a day where there is no wind at all? No matter how aggressively you pull that string, or like a crazed person, run from one side of the field to the other, it will not stay in the air. What's missing? A gust of wind, of course! We need wind resistance because that provides the air drag needed to keep the kite in the air. The more resistance, the higher it flies.

Same thing with volunteer leadership. Outsiders or team members who voice resistance to your vision can help you see things you may not see. Resistance can help teams reach new heights. Sometimes resistance or opposition exposes holes in your plan. You may have to change the plan, change directions. Embrace the fight! If they are right about the plan, change it, move on, and be prepared to fight a different battle. Effective volunteer leaders know, "you can always change the fight, but don't fight the change."

Watch For The Alligators

On every path there will be submerged threats, like alligators. They become apparent when you "step" on them. Simply take time to understand the meanings behind these potential threats:

Insider threats - Like the music group "The Undisputed Truth" sang in their 1971 hit song, "Smiling faces . . . show no traces, of the evil that lurks within." No one can hurt us more than those close to us. People, even family members, smile and pat us on the back. But, oh boy, step on their feelings and they are ready to snap. These are the insider threats. It's common to experience this behavior. Understanding the why, however, can avoid hurt feelings or adverse behavior that may occur.

Malicious threats - Some people volunteer for all the wrong reasons. They volunteer but don't commit 100%. They may view your success as a way of sabotaging their personal plans or "stealing their thunder." Things may simply not be going their way. Who knows? Maybe they wanted to be the leader and now are resentful that someone has taken the role. Hence, they may go to great lengths to sabotage the person taking the lead.

Unintended threats - People don't know what they don't know. Some team members may not have the skills to contribute, so they do nothing to help. It is not their intention to sabotage anyone. They may simply be unprepared or not yet ready to serve in a particular role. No leader, team member, or anyone for that matter, is always ready to serve. It is rare to find that "perfect" volunteer. We all make mistakes. In fact if you do find someone on your team who IS perfect, you may want to excuse them from the team. Otherwise, he or she may hinder the process of learning through your mistakes!

Don't Take It Personally

The best advice any mentor has given; "Don't take any action as a personal attack." Yes, this approach can be difficult to take. Even when it appears to be a personal attack, take the high road! Achieve your goal out of pure determination. As they say, success is the best revenge! Normalize the threat or malicious behavior as part of the journey. Volunteer leaders reach their goals faster by recognizing the threat, addressing the adverse behavior sooner than later, and then seeking to understand the other person's position. Seeking to understand the opposite side can diminish the power and fear of a personal attack. Once understood, a volunteer leader can then communicate how or why the adverse behavior is detrimental to the team. Help team members resolve their issues and become the winners you know they can be..

Reaching an understanding could help resolve an issue quickly and create a winning result. Reaching a consensus can help move the team forward or, in some cases, prevent good team members from leaving the team. An effective way for a volunteer leader to reach a consensus with a team member is to expose any hidden agendas someone may have.

People can have hidden agendas. Understanding this became all too clear when I came across a book decades ago called "Messages: The Communication Book", (McKay, Davis, Fanning, 2009). Oh boy. This book should be a must-read for every person serving in management and leadership. Often, as the book describes, people will communicate in a way that disguises their real intent. Some team members keep the leader from seeing their true feelings. Their thinking all have the same theme; I'm Better, I'm Good, I know more or I'm helpless, I'm blameless; just to name a few. Uncovering these real feelings can save your volunteering life. On the other hand, as a volunteer leader, look at your actions and determine if you are disguising hidden messages. Instead of thinking "I know it all," learn to think, "I can listen, be interested, and ask questions." Instead of blaming others or expressing "It's not my fault," learn to find a new position: "Nobody's perfect. Decisions I make as a leader can sometimes contribute to things going wrong."

Know that responsibility as a leader genuinely means "I am Response-Able." Practice being more open with your team members. Being vulnerable can be an asset. It is said that perfect vulnerability is actually perfect strength. Learn how to know yourself better. There are numerous leadership assessments that can be taken online to better know your strengths and opportunities for growth. As you become more comfortable opening up and sharing your weaknesses and need for support, your team will respond in kind. Your team members will open up to you when you learn to open up to them! Be the winner they want you to be.

WE'RE ALL JUST CRACKED POTS
(An old folktale from India)

Once upon a time, there was a water bearer in India, who for many years delivered water in two large pots on a pole carried across the back of his neck. One pot was perfect, the other had a crack in it. After each day, the water bearer noticed the perfect pot always delivered a full portion of water, while the cracked pot leaked water and delivered only a half portion. (According to the tale these pots could talk to the water bearer.)

The perfect pot expressed pride in its accomplishment to always deliver a full pot of water. The cracked pot, however, felt ashamed of it's imperfection, as on a daily basis it only accomplished half of its chosen purpose. After some time, the cracked pot apologized to the water bearer for being unable to deliver a full load because of the crack. Feeling sorry for the cracked pot, the water bearer retraced his daily walk to show something to the pot. As they walked back along the path the cracked pot noticed beautiful flowers on one side of the path. The water bearer said to the cracked pot, "Notice there are flowers only on your side of the path and not the other. I've always known about your flaw and I took advantage of it by planting seeds on your side of the path. And every day you've watered them." The water bearer expressed that this was where he picked the beautiful flowers he took up the hill to decorate his master's house.

Moral of the story: No one is perfect. We all have flaws. Have a winning mindset. We may be cracked pots, but our flaws can turn out to be a blessing in disguise. Among your team members, even the character flaws that appear to be obstacles can turn out to be character assets that build you as a leader.

"There are people who have nuclear bomb potential, but are just living a firecracker life!"

- Pastor Jim Reeves, Faith Community Church

DISCIPLINE #2:

FIND YOUR WHY, FIND SUCCESS

Countless studies report that the number of people volunteering has been steadily declining for years, even decades. Volunteer team members may not seem engaged. Some proponents assert this is happening because volunteers don't see the why!

Simon Sinek is a British-American author and motivational speaker. He is known for popularizing the concept of The Golden Circle and the book "Start With Why." He advocates creating a culture of finding what inspires people and leaders. As he illustrates on the circles of a "bullseye" target, what creates a culture of success (as with Apple, Google, or Nike) is "The Why." Everyone knows "what they do" and "how they do it," he illustrates. But only a few organizations hit the bullseye to clarify "why they do what they do." He says when you think, act and communicate starting with Why, you can inspire others.

German philosopher Frederick Nietzsche said, "He who has a *why* can endure any *how*." He referenced that "Knowing your why is an important first step in figuring out how to achieve the goals that excite you . . ." Nothing is more powerful or motivating than when a volunteer leader determines "why" he or she wants to be a leader. Author and motivational speaker Eric Thomas shared his feelings about one of the biggest upsets in the boxing world:

> "'Iron' Mike Tyson was hailed as the fiercest boxer the world had ever known. Nobody who ever got knocked out by Mike Tyson ever got back up, except for one fighter named Buster Douglas. In the 1990 championship boxing match, Iron Mike floored Buster Douglas with his signature uppercut power punch. It was almost a ten count before Douglas was saved by the bell. What happened next shocked the world. Buster came back and knocked out Mike Tyson! Reporters asked Buster Douglas, "What happened?" Douglas said: "Listen to me, it's real simple. Before my mother died, she told the whole world that I was going to beat Mike Tyson. Two days before the fight my mother died." It's simply because Buster's 'Why' was greater than that punch, his 'Why' was greater than defeat . . . if you don't know what your 'Why' is, and your 'Why' isn't strong, you're gonna get knocked out every single day."

One of the most challenging life adventures a volunteer leader can have is to employ his or her skills to help others find success. Finding your WHY can make all the difference in the world and open doors to personal development.

My wife and I attend Faith Community Church. We were attracted and inspired by Pastor Jim Reeve's transparent and straightforward teachings on becoming not just a Christian leader, but just being a better Christian, a better human being. We would often hear him say, "there are so many talented human beings living their lives based on negative belief systems that tell them they are not wealthy or successful enough to make a difference in the world." Volunteer leaders who want to ensure success can learn from other leaders, even leaders from the past. In a speech delivered by the first black South African President, Nelson Mandela, he quoted a now-famous heartfelt passage written by Marianne Williamson in her book, "A Return to Love:"

Our worst fear . . . is not that we are inadequate. Our deepest fear is that we are powerful beyond measure! It is our Light, not our darkness that frightens us. But if we let our Light shine we unconsciously give other people permission to do the same. And as we are liberated from our own fears, our presence automatically liberates others.

The message here?: Find the magic that will unleash your light and your greatness! There is "nuclear bomb" potential in discovering your why! Finding your why can create clarity in your ability to help others find their why and lead them to their purpose.

The WIIFM

One method of finding your own "why" can be through leading and mentoring; helping volunteers find their WIIFM, **What's In It For Me**? Successful volunteer leaders are driven to nurture relationships with others. They focus on finding people's WIIFM. Helping team members find their why will lead your team to great success every time. Instead of asking a potential candidate to volunteer for a project, try showing how he or she could benefit from the experience. Creating WIIFM questions and statements is one of the most effective ways to encourage and recruit volunteers.

Here is a WIIFM conversation for someone who needs a reason to take public speaking classes:

Opening WIIFM Question: "Have you ever thought of taking a course to learn public speaking?"

Supporting WIIFM Statement: "90% of the top money makers in this country have one thing in common; they are great public speakers."

WIIFM Call to Action: "Taking this course will help make you a better public speaker!"

Growing to become a successful volunteer leader means doing the work and making a difference. Imagine making a difference in the lives of others through helping them find their WIIFM.

In the 1990s, Michael Josephson, a law professor who founded The Josephson Institute and hosted his KNXT 1070 news radio segment called "Character Counts," told a story about Harry Shabazian, a teacher in East Los Angeles who worked with "at risk" youths. Josephson described these youth as having learning and behavioral issues impeding their ability to finish school and make a decent life for themselves. In 1989, Shabazian challenged a few of these students to train with him to run the Los Angeles Marathon. Josephson shared that "after accepting the challenge and months of training the students completed the grueling 26-mile run." He explained that it started what was known as "Students Run L.A.," an intervention program for at-risk youths in Los Angeles schools.

Josephson illustrated in his radio segment that when these youngsters finished the race they were filled with a great sense of accomplishment, and felt they could succeed in other aspects of their lives. He said of the 2,000 kids who finished the L.A. marathon in 2001, most of them stayed in school and avoided gangs. Ninety percent (90%) of those youngsters graduated from high school and three-quarters attended post-secondary education. Josephson illustrated that Shabazian made a difference in the lives of others by discovering what would be in it for those at-risk kids.

Maslow's Hierarchy of Needs

Another way volunteer leaders can successfully help develop their teams is to first understand what team members truly value. During many years as a volunteer youth coach, I discovered this understanding through working alongside volunteer parents. One of these parents (who we will call Mr. Doe), was an exceptional coach. As a single parent, he talked about his quest to be more confident. He wanted to work with young people and earn school tuition credit for his time spent coaching the kids. His communication and coaching style was spot on. When he was at basketball practice our team's players practiced longer and stayed engaged. They shot the ball better. They hustled better. They became better pupils of the game. There was one little problem though. Mr. Doe would miss a great number of practices and even missed some of the early season competitions.

Weeks had passed before he finally approached me and explained, "Sorry, Mr. Kitchen," holding his head down. "My son and I are looking for a stable place to live." We came to find out he and his son were practically homeless. For him, looking for housing throughout the weeks was more urgent than attending the practices. It became obvious that Mr. Doe needed to satisfy his basic need for shelter before addressing his need to participate in social activities. Ultimately, once his problem was discovered, the school's church helped him and his son find consistent room and board. He began attending practices regularly and was instrumental in helping our team reach the playoffs.

This story illustrates Maslow's Hierarchy of Needs, a theory psychologist Abraham Maslow developed in the 1940s to explain individual development and motivation. Maslow pointed out that all humans act in a way that will address their basic needs before moving on to satisfy other higher-level needs. Maslow represented his theory as a hierarchical triangle. It showed how basic needs must be met before one can "climb" the hierarchy to address social and self-fulfillment needs. He described these needs in this order, [Figure 1 - from bottom to top]: **Physiological** (such as hunger, thirst, and sleep), **Safety** (security, protection from danger, and freedom from pain), **Social** (friendship, giving and receiving love, engaging in social activities) **Esteem** (self-respect, self-confidence, and recognition and achievement), and **Self-actualization** (the desire to develop and realize your full potential). Some experts may conclude that Knowledge (Information) has become a vital need within this structure.

Maslow's Hierarchy of Needs

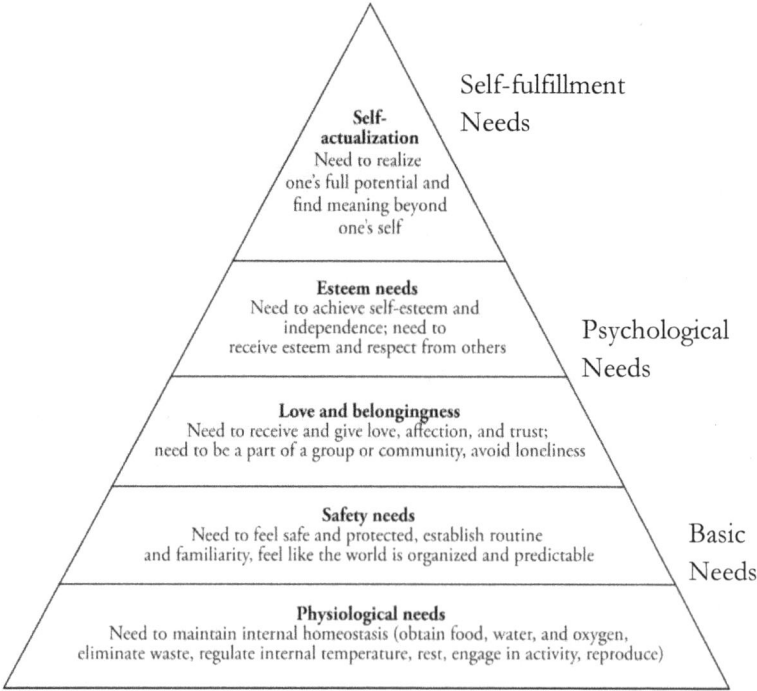

Self-fulfillment Needs

Self-actualization
Need to realize one's full potential and find meaning beyond one's self

Esteem needs
Need to achieve self-esteem and independence; need to receive esteem and respect from others

Psychological Needs

Love and belongingness
Need to receive and give love, affection, and trust; need to be a part of a group or community, avoid loneliness

Safety needs
Need to feel safe and protected, establish routine and familiarity, feel like the world is organized and predictable

Basic Needs

Physiological needs
Need to maintain internal homeostasis (obtain food, water, and oxygen, eliminate waste, regulate internal temperature, rest, engage in activity, reproduce)

Figure 1 – Maslow's Hierarchy Triangle

Understanding and employing Maslow's principle can lead to finding undisputed success recognizing your team's needs. It is critical to determine a volunteer's true availability and readiness to serve. This can save valuable time for the volunteer leader and ensure that the volunteer would be more fully invested.

But what's the secret to finding the right person for the team? One secret lies in discovering a person's readiness. The other is discovering what he or she values. Can it be that simple? Sure it can! When people see the value of pursuing their own purpose, it isn't hard for them to decide to join a successful team. Help people find their "why."

Successful leaders can accomplish any goal when they organize a team of volunteers who know their why, are ready to engage and whose values are in alignment with each other. There must be a benefit and motivation for any person to sacrifice their time, efforts, and energy to ensure the leader and team succeeds. But, that is not enough. The other part of this involves understanding relationships.

In Toastmasters International, volunteer leaders learn the art of communication and leadership. Members become better leaders through event planning; team building; and hosting club, area, and division speech competitions. It takes weeks, even months to plan a competition. Waiting to the last week or few days can be disastrous. If, however, a volunteer has strong personal relations with people, it is possible to turn a seemingly impossible task into a successful one. Here's an example:

One day, I received a call from Maria, one of the contest chairpersons. She asked me about getting help to organize her contest event.

"No problem," I said, "I can help. What day is the event on?"

After a long, uncomfortable pause, she said, "In 10 days!"

15

"Do you have a venue yet," I asked. She replied, "Well, no, do you have ideas?"

Initially, a thought came to me to simply hang up the phone and pretend we lost connection. I felt compassionate, however, remembering when I, too, had been in that exact position.

"Should I cancel?" she asked. I expressed, "Let's see what we can do!"

Boy did we learn something, even as seasoned district officers. After a few calls to some of our colleagues and friends, I encountered many of the same responses:

"Wow, for Maria, anything!" many members expressed. "All she needed to do was just call and ask!"

In less than 10 days, we found a venue at no cost, three of the five needed club contestants, someone to make fliers to promote the event, contest facilitators, a registration team, and food for the event (under $100). On the day of the event, over 70 people attended!

How was that possible? This surely went beyond just helping people find their WIIFM, right?. This was only possible through understanding the power of relationships!

Maria and I learned a valuable lesson about relationships. We called everyone she personally knew or had helped. Maria "deposited" a lot of her time helping others. One of our close leadership colleagues, Joan, would always preach to her volunteer team members, "you must make deposits before you can make withdrawals." It's like an ATM machine; you can't make a request for money if you put no money in! The same goes for relationships. If a volunteer leader has not taken time to put in the work to help others, it's nearly impossible to request others to withdraw time out of their schedules to help you! Helping others is one of the keys to attaining undisputable success. You help somebody, they help you. Think of it as the "Rule of Reciprocity." Maria, over the years, had helped so many people with their events and contests that when she called them for help, without blinking an eye, people came to her aid. They knew their "why."

One of the greatest assets a volunteer leader can ever acquire is learning to be a servant leader, giving your time to serve others. When you serve others and give your time, it shows them you value them and what they do for the organization. Furthermore, they will nearly always be there for you when you need them. Bottom line, people need to feel appreciated. In other words, to see the WIIFM, they must see the value in volunteering.

Our jobs as volunteer leaders is to help our team members understand this principle. Why would some volunteers spend only two hours a week volunteering, yet others will spend 40 hours a week? Let's face it. Would you give up three weekends each month for six months, or even a year, to volunteer for an organization? You might if you see the value in doing so; especially if that value is in alignment with your personal vision for your life.

Values help develop a clearer sense of what's most important to you in life. Some values jump right out to you: learning new skills, overcoming a fear, being acknowledged, contributing to a cause, achieving greater education, or simply wanting to make a difference in the world.

Value-driven leadership is the best way to describe it. Simply put, value is the worth of something based on what is important to your team members. Discovering WIIFMs and utilizing value-driven leadership can ignite a person to volunteer at the drop of a dime.

Now you are probably asking, "How does a leader discover what is important to a potential volunteer?" Glad you asked.

One amazing method is through the process of discovering, uncovering, and asking questions. This is what we sometimes call "peeling the onion." Ever peel an onion layer by layer? Did it make your eyes irritable? Did you start to tear up?

Uncovering people's values can lead to the same result. The more you peel, the closer you get to people's core purpose. And the closer you get to their core purpose, the more they begin to show their emotions. People can get emotional when they discover their purpose; what they have been longing to do with their lives. Uncovering the "tears" or "emotional driving forces" can be the key to discovering what will make your team members leap into action. And understand the motivation and needs of your team members has little to do with your need. They want to know that you care about what they care about. They want to know how you can help them accomplish their goal(s). You've heard the saying, no one cares what you know . . . until they know that you care.

How about this example? Why would a student take out a $75,000 student loan to earn a Bachelor's degree at a for-profit school for three years versus investing only $40,000 at a traditional school for four to five years? Doesn't make sense, huh? Of course there is the possibility that the student may not have the grade point average (GPA) required to get into a traditional school. But what if the student did have the required GPA, along with a financial aid plan to pay for the schooling? Surely the prospective student would choose the traditional school, right? Not necessarily. It may be that the student sees more value in getting a degree faster, thus getting into the work force faster than it would take if attending a traditional school. Earning and receiving a Bachelor's degree in Accounting and potentially making $40,000 a year within three years might be preferable to taking up to five years or longer to attain the same degree and employment. The potential of receiving two years of a $40K per year salary versus not receiving those earnings at all if still in school. It all boils down to knowing the "why!"

Help people discover what is important to them and watch them act with great urgency. Volunteer leaders hear a lot of concerns like, "I can't find people to volunteer! I get nothing but objections." How can a volunteer leader overcome these objections? First, try to understand what is a true objection versus a "smoke screen." An objection is a real barrier preventing a volunteer from participating or accomplishing a task (lack of knowledge, no transportation, work schedule, baby-sitter issues). Smoke screens are just excuses! "I don't have time," "I need more time," "I can't do that." Learn to remove the smoke screens and barriers by asking questions: Why...? What if...? Have you ever...? Get them to visualize their goal. Paint the picture for them. People can achieve ANYTHING if the leader can be a resource to help them to achieve success. Show them how to make it happen.

Another tool you can use as a volunteer leader to help others is to tell your own story or experience. Share with them your common goals and challenges. Telling your story helps potential volunteers and team members discover and uncover their own truths and values. Driving your team to take action based on their values is the key. People don't always respond to what you say but to how they feel about what you say. As quoted by writers and authors (Carl Buechner, Maya Angelou, Carol Buchner and others) "people will forget the things you do, and the things you say, but they will never forget how you made them feel."

Years of leading as a volunteer leader have uncovered many common reasons that prevent volunteer leaders from accomplishing a goal:

- Requests of the team or members are ambiguous
- Volunteers are uncertain they will get full support
- The volunteer leader doesn't address the objections
- The leader avoids covering the WIIFM/values
- Value is not perceived by team members

It helps when the volunteer leader is very clear on what needs to be done. As a volunteer leader, ask yourself, "What is it that I want members to take action on?" "When do I want them to take action on it?" "How important is it to these members?"

A volunteer leader can lead any team to accomplish a goal by understanding and executing a plan that gives team members what they need. Here is a guide that may help decipher or uncover hidden concerns expressed by members:

IF (Team Member):	THEN (Volunteer Leader):
Needs help with task	Provides resources & support
Lacks motivation	Shows benefit of taking action
Is unclear about role(s)	Clearly describe features of task
Disagrees with goal(s)	Explain the benefits & end results
Looking for WIIFM	Show reasons for performing task

Recruiting The Right People For The Right Job

My friend Carol is a business owner. She volunteers her time for a non-profit communication organization and serves on leadership teams to, in turn, enhance her communication skills. Volunteers know her for her time-management skills and strong ability to lead. On a Monday morning she received a call from a team leader that sounded like this:

"Hi Carol. This is Susan. Thanks for serving as our registration chair for our fundraising event. Do you have any people on your team yet? Do you have any questions?"

Carol was befuddled. Why? Because, she didn't actually volunteer to serve as a chairperson. She was volunteered. Ever experience that feeling? It happens regularly in volunteer organizations.

Authentic recruitment is critical to getting the right people for the right team for the right task at the right time. There are times when the pressure is on a volunteer leader to recruit a team quickly. They begin to look for those who can join the team and accomplish the task. Sometimes leaders are just looking for warm bodies to fill open positions, just to say "yeah, I got my team in place!" The only problem is, the leader never officially asked them for permission until after submitting their name on the team. Let's face it, many of us have done it.

Volunteer vs. Voluntold

There is a running joke in volunteer organizations about how people get selected for a team. You may have heard comments like these:

"I missed one team meeting and came back to learn I'm now the chairperson?"

"How did I get on the food committee? I've been out of town. And, I hate serving food!"

"Well, I was talking to Jessica. She told me I would be working on the conference committee. I had no idea!"

Volunteer leaders must discipline themselves to understand there is little good that comes from volunteering people without their permission. It undermines your relationship with people and hurts your credibility as a leader. In the long run, you may lose team members who never committed in the first place.

Urban dictionaries and terminology define this method as being "voluntold," the combination between "volunteered" and "told." It happens often in the nonprofit and corporate world, even among families for that matter. People find themselves voluntold for numerous tasks by their bosses, spouses, and friends. Sometimes, it's disguised as a "suggestion." Why do some volunteer leaders, even managers, do this? Often, to meet a deadline. Perhaps it's "crunch time." The leader must accomplish a goal and needs a definite "go to" person who can make it happen. Perhaps it's a person they know they have a close relationship with who won't mind being asked at the last minute. Sometimes, it can just come from having a prior conversation with someone looking for a chance to get involved. And then, when the opportunity suddenly arises, the leader knows who to call or "volunteer." Is there a difference between being volunteered versus being voluntold? Sure. At least when voluntold, the person is told about it and stands a chance to say yes or no!

Whatever name it goes by, it is possible "volun-telling" people can ruin their ambitions for wanting to volunteer. Volunteers who were voluntold often lack commitment, which often hinders a team's performance. Sure, the team members show up for meetings and tasks, but they are not effective because they were unwillingly pressured or hoodwinked into participating. Recruiting is the only way a volunteer leader can build a high-performance team. Here are some tips on recruiting and building your team:

- Look for volunteers early as possible. Why? Because every other leader is looking for the same good volunteer you are looking for.
- Be clear and straightforward in asking a person to serve on your team. Tell him or her precisely what you want them to do.
- Reach out for referrals or recommendations. Be open minded.
- You pick your own team. Don't let others dictate who will be on your team. Be aware of why others want to pick your team.
- Avoid choosing only friends or those who you only get along with. Look for diversity in knowledge and experience.
- Don't purely rely only on experience! Sometimes inexperienced volunteers who are driven to succeed will do a better job.

Experience Doesn't Mean Success

There is a myth some volunteer leaders buy into: "Recruit experienced people if you want the task done right!" That is not necessarily so, as discovered in a "Volunteer Impact MBA Survey" conducted in 2016. The hypotheses were 1) Organizations can predict volunteers who always accomplish tasks, and 2) Volunteer experience or time determines whether tasks get accomplished. The study, through a survey of volunteers, proved these hypotheses wrong and discovered the following:

- Volunteers accomplished 100% of their assigned tasks whether they spent 1-5 hours or 15-24 hours weekly.
- Volunteers with 1-2 years' experience accomplished 100% of their tasks equally as successful as volunteers with 10 years' experience.
- Of those who accomplished 100% of their assigned tasks, 90% indicated they were given adequate time, and 80% were given adequate resources to accomplish their tasks.
- There was no correlation or significance to accomplishing tasks based on experience or hours spent on the task.

Want volunteers who can successfully accomplish tasks? Help them find their "why" and then give them the support and tools to find success.

"If everything is coming at you too fast, you're in the wrong lane!"

-Anonymous

DISCIPLINE #3:

STAY FOCUSED, STAY IN YOUR LANE

In almost every company or organization, volunteers must multi-task. Sometimes, volunteer leaders can inadvertently meddle in other projects. Sometimes leaders will experience scenarios like the one described below:

Eric and Rosalyn are exemplary volunteer leaders. They have chaired many committees together. Last year, Eric chaired the business conference meeting and did a great job. Members have expressed wanting to use some of his ideas for the future conferences. This year, Eric is chairing a different team, the registration team. Rosalyn, on the other hand, is chairing the business conference meeting. She has been enthusiastically meeting with her team about the planning and implementation. In a follow-up meeting, she observed the venue setup was different than what was agreed upon by the team. In fact, two of her team members questioned her direction on the project. When she inquired why, the team members voiced, "Eric met with us. He showed us how he organized the tables and registration. He recommended that we should continue to arrange it the same way!" Rosalyn seemed a bit upset and confused. After all, Eric was assigned to a completely different team project.

One of the biggest stumbling blocks to our success as a volunteer leader is the ambiguity or misunderstanding on "who is doing what." This happens often in organizations. It is ideal for every volunteer leader to focus on his or her team's project. We call this staying in your lane. When meeting with team members, it is beneficial for the leader to provide clear guidance. Help keep volunteers focused on "their lane." Help them be aware that others may drift into their lane and distract the team from accomplishing their task. Understanding this principle can save time and energy and create better harmony amongst the team.

Effective volunteer leaders know helping members stay in their lane prevents duplication of efforts. Keeping team members focused ensures that tasks get done and eliminates friction on the team.

To plan a typical one or two-day business conference, it may take a large team, anywhere from 120 to 150 volunteers. To organize registration and hospitality activities alone could take a minimum of 30 volunteers. And with event planning comes the inevitable need to make changes to the plan. Team members may overhear what other teams are doing, second guess their own efforts, and begin focusing on tasks not relevant to their project. It's a good idea to check what others have done or review how other teams are progressing. If, however, changes to a plan are imminent, ensure that the decision to change is relevant. And don't be afraid to change directions or make the tough decisions. This is part of a volunteer leader's role.

Making a clear, timely decision is the hallmark of a successful volunteer leader. A visionary person may see the change needed, but a leader must decide. Don't be quick to make unfounded decisions. Weigh out all feedback and evidence and make a sound decision.

Imagine driving your car to an out-of-town meeting, one you have spent a great deal of time and energy mapping out. Somehow, to make up time you decide to take a shortcut. In doing so you reach a road that dead ends at a cliff. You wouldn't continue to drive forward over the cliff, would you? It would be obvious that you would need to turn around and go back the other way. Oddly, though, some might indeed drive off the cliff. Others may stop the car, get out and spend unnecessary time trying to figure out what happened and what to do next.

The same applies in being a volunteer leader. To reach success leaders need to make decisions. Knowing your leadership style can help determine the expediency with which you turn around to take a different road. This requires knowing what kind of thinker you are, or what type of leadership style you possess. Trust me, there are always times when volunteer leaders must take a different road.

Discovering your leadership style is a critical advantage. This can help to establish clear direction and drive your team in the direction intended. A solid recommendation is to learn what type of leader are you? Different tasks require different leadership styles. If one style is not working, switch to a style that may create better success. Are you a Hands-on Leader, fully assuming the leadership role while at the same time rolling up your sleeves and working side-by-side with the team? Or, are you a Figurehead Leader who just holds the title of "leader" but rarely, if ever, helps to make things happen? Perhaps your style represents that of a Micromanager who controls every thought, decision, or action. Or do you prefer to be a transformational leader who emphasizes the importance of growing and working through team collaboration? Knowing your leadership style(s) can help determine ways to help your team.

Let's go back to making that business trip. You may be puzzled as to why you suddenly got on the wrong road in the first place. Surely, you saw other drivers taking the same road. Ever thought to ask, "hmm, why am I following them when I clearly mapped out my own plans?" Sometimes we are unclear about our own decisions. And then we focus so much on what others are doing that we forget to pay attention to our own plans.

Learn to stay in your lane and help your team members do the same. Practicing discipline in this area will pay handsomely. Focus on your part and help others focus on theirs. Sure, observing what other teams are doing can help, but stay focused on your primary plan. It is hard to stay in your lane when you are looking everywhere else.

Learning to stay in your lane can also lead a volunteer leader to another valuable skill set: the ability to recognize and assign tasks based on an individual's talent. Different people bring different skillsets to the team. This unveils a significant revelation: every team member can have an equal share of responsibility but not be equal in talent. Some team members possess a high emotional intelligence and are able to use emotional information to guide their thinking and behavior. Some people are analytical thinkers and strongly supportive of policies and procedures. Maximizing a volunteer leader's opportunity for success means understanding that every person is different.

This brings up an intriguing question. Shouldn't everyone be treated equal? That question was posed to Ms. Lydia Boyd, Distinguished Toastmaster and Past International Director in Toastmasters International, a not-for-profit organization. District Governors (now called District Directors) dream of leading their District to becoming number one in the world. Today there are 100 Districts serving more than 350,000 members worldwide. As District Governor in 1989, Boyd led her Southern California District to #1 district in the world. How did she do it? Boyd makes two points: 1) treating people fairly, and 2) ensuring all team members contributed to overall goal. She explained:

> *"I was once asked, 'Do you treat everyone the same?'*
> *The answer is 'No!' It depends on the person and/or the*
> *situation. I lead, educate, or accept the experience of*

others. No matter the type of leadership skills used, respect for others is always first in mind. When you show respect for other leaders who have integrity, you will receive respect. Always be willing to listen to others. Be honest in everything you say and do. And if you don't know what is best, don't be afraid to ask questions!"

Solid advice coming from a seasoned volunteer leader who puts people first. The second point Ms. Boyd asserted was to, "Get everyone involved. Every person can take on a small role as part of the big picture." This illustrates a very effective way of accomplishing undisputed success. Break down big tasks into very small chunks. This can also help keep team members focused on their individual tasks. Giving a team member a task that's too large for them to handle can lead them to reach too far outside their scope (or lane).

It is far more effective to tackle one big project by breaking it down into small tasks and assigning the right roles to the right people. Have you ever put together a 1,000-piece puzzle? With so many pieces and colors, how do you know what pieces fit where? A good puzzle master knows to assemble a huge puzzle one section at a time. All the red pieces go together, and then all the green pieces and finally all the blue pieces. When all these small sections of the puzzle are connected, we can finally visualize a bright red barn nestled in a wide-open area of green grass under a beautiful blue sky. Sure, lots of pieces to put together, but each piece has a role. Coach members to stay focused on their "pieces," their task, their role. Once each task is complete, the tasks are then connected to complete one huge project.

The truth is, everyone and anyone can play a vital role in accomplishing a team goal. It may be a major role, it may be a small role, but every role is important to the outcome. No one is ever too small to be effective . . . if they learn to stay in their lane.

"Anyone who has never made a mistake, has never tried anything new."

- Albert Einstein.

DISCIPLINE #4:

FAILURE IS SUCCESS IN DISGUISE

Don't be afraid of failure! It is part of the learning process. Albert Einstein had a steadfast perception and many expressions on what can be best described as "failing forward." As babies, we crawl, we stand, we stumble, we fall. We go through life and pass up countless opportunities simply because of the fear of failure. As Einstein expressed, "Opportunity is missed by most because it's dressed in overalls and looks like work."

There's a similar misconception about failure; it is actually success in progress! For a volunteer leader who wishes to reach undisputed success, it is critical to know and accept that failure is part of the learning orientation. Our failures become a catalyst for learning, for change, for development and personal growth. It's always better to give things a try and risk failing than to not try at all.

Leading in a volunteer organization presents the perfect platform to learn from mistakes. Volunteer leaders can only learn from what failure has to teach us if we're willing to embrace the failure and learn from it. When willing to accept

31

the fact that failure occurs, we receive the positive lessons failure teaches:

- Failure teaches us that success — real success — rarely comes in the form of a "big break." More often than not it comes after months, even years, of hard work.
- Failure teaches us to try many avenues before giving up, as there is more than one way to succeed.
- Failure helps to narrow down and eliminate processes that do not work and gets us closer to our success.

It is written that Thomas Edison's teachers said he was "too stupid to learn anything." He was fired from his first two jobs for being "non-productive." As an inventor, Edison made 1,000 unsuccessful attempts at inventing the light bulb. When asked how he felt about failing so much, he replied, "I have not failed. I've just found 1,000 ways that didn't work." Edison believed that many of life's failures are people not realizing how close they were to success and simply giving up.

Successful volunteer leaders discipline their mindset to understand there will be both success and failures. The faster they see something that doesn't work, the closer they get to the solution. Ponder this notion. It's like looking for a set of keys that have gone missing. Ever noticed they are always found in the last place we look? The only unknown is the amount of time it will take to find them. And what do we do when we don't find those keys for which we have searched hundreds of times? We move on and buy a replacement set!

The same discipline can be applied as a volunteer leader if their team fails to hit the goal the first or second time. The sooner you realize a process doesn't work, the sooner you can move on!

From experience, however, it is possible to avoid the pitfalls of making the same mistakes over and over again. Simply stop reinventing the wheel. Insight and feedback may show you that a seemingly impossible task has been accomplished before. Experience is a great teacher. Work smarter and not harder. Embrace failure as a learning point. Use what has worked in the past, but always realize you can make it better.

Developing A Learning Orientation To Life

Learning to accept "failure" as part of the learning experience is critical to teaching volunteers to develop a learning orientation.

Long ago, a young gentleman named Marcus volunteered as a youth basketball coach. His 10-year-old son, Marquis, played basketball in the Catholic Youth Organization (CYO). Marcus began volunteering as a youth coach to become part of his son's experience in the game. Marcus was also a youth coach at the local parks & recreation program and was more familiar with coaching rules at the parks. There, competitiveness and winning were the primary driving forces.

However, Marcus had been advised that the CYO program was based on the principles of playing as Christians on the field. CYO rules and regulations promoted sportsmanship over winning.

It was important for Marcus to recognize, as a volunteer leader, the opportunity to understand and coach others on the importance of the organization's purpose and goals. He needed to shift his learning orientation.

Society makes us feel like failures if we don't "win the prize." Yet navigating through the journey of learning from failure is one of the greatest orientations a volunteer leader can go through.

The process of learning through failure has created the best leaders the world has ever known. Abraham Lincoln failed numerous times; losing jobs, losing a wife, and losing races to become House speaker and U.S. Senator before becoming the 16th President of the United States. Founder of Microsoft Bill Gates failed to follow in his father's footstep as a lawyer, failed in his first business venture with his original computer idea, and dropped out of Harvard before successfully launching and sustaining the Microsoft Company. Michael Jordan, who is credited saying, "I've missed more than 9000 shots…lost almost 300 games…26 times [was] trusted to take the game-winning shot and missed." He was once passed up for the varsity basketball team. Yet he went on to win six NBA championship titles; 3 championships back to back - twice!

Every successful team has to learn the discipline of handling failure. Developing effective volunteer orientations can help new volunteers understand the organization and perform their roles successfully. When this discipline is skipped, volunteers often just perceive that failure is a bad thing. In turn, they don't return to volunteer, let alone to serve as a volunteer leader.

It is good to develop a two-part learning orientation. The first part is to orient volunteers on the important aspects of the organization:

- How does your organization do business?
- What kind of support is given?
- What are general expectations of the leaders? The volunteer?
- What is the history of the organization, its mission and goals?
- Is there a volunteer training and meeting schedule?

The second part is to determine how your team members will develop the necessary skills to accomplish the task. Showing and telling are just two ways to make this happen. The better learning orientation involves both. We call this "experiential learning." We tell members what is needed, we show them how to do it, and then we allow them to show and tell us.

Here is what the process looks like:

We Do, They Watch - Leader shows, member observes.
We Do, They Help - Leader guides, member participates.
They Do, We Help - Member guides, leader participates.
They Do, We Watch - Member shows, leader observes.

Knowledge can also cross over from skills learned from other fields. One of my early career aspirations was to become a news media journalist. Graduating with a degree in Journalism, and subsequently landing some small reporter and columnist jobs, I later discovered that being a journalist was not my passion. But the skills I learned and employ as a leader today are priceless. Journalists, as well as investigators, utilize a journalistic technique to develop leads. This proven technique involves asking open-ended questions whose answers are considered basic in information gathering and problem solving. These are called the five W's; *Who*, *What*, *Where*, *When* and *Why*. An additional element is the *How* (we'll get to that in a moment). Aside from what we call "feature" articles, the five W's are prominent in the lead of every news-style article; Who did What, When, Where, and Why? The How part always provides in-depth coverage.

Now, why do I mention this? Well, a good volunteer leader can employ this same thought process when developing the scope of a project. This process is almost guaranteed to help any volunteer leader attain clarity and undisputed success.

Here are examples of some relevant questions:
What - What needs to be done? What is the bottom-line goal, the mission? What do I want each member to do? What resources do we have? What should be done if a member doesn't contribute?
Who - Who can help? Who is capable, available, and willing to serve on the team?
Where - Where can I find members for my team? Where

can we find monies for the project? **When** - When does the task need to be accomplished? When will our team meetings be held? When should I change the game plan or a team member if needed? **Why** - Why are we doing this? Why would a team member get involved?

Once a volunteer leader knows the 5 W's and the mission, he or she can plan the How:
How - How do we accomplish the goal? How do we communicate with each other? How do we work as a team? How do we get the resources needed? How do I, as the volunteer leader, keep each person focused?

Volunteer leaders who can answer these questions in a clear manner can always see their vision and help their team exceed any expectations. Excuse me. Did someone say, "exceed expectations?"

How do the great leaders exceed expectations? Well, don't laugh at this analogy, but if you have ever seen the animated movie, "The Lion King 3", you'd understand. In this adventure there is a scene where a meerkat named Timon encounters a wise spiritual baboon named Rafiki. Timon explains he is looking for a beautiful place where he doesn't have to hide from the dangers of the jungle. But all Timon sees are jungle trees. The wise baboon, Rafiki, takes his yoga position, legs folded, hands poised, eyes closed, and explains, "To find it, you must look beyond what you see!" Now, many of us would respond the way Timon did, "What the heck does that mean? How do we do that?"

Look at it this way. If we focus on what we see, that is what we get. However, by being open minded with an unjaded thought process and the right capabilities, a volunteer leader can tap into his or her imagination and team members' capabilities to uncover ways to not just achieve the goal but exceed it. This is what defines the "How." How can we reach outside what we see? Well, if your team can increase the organization's membership by 3% with new members from solely one city, what can the team accomplish by visiting other cities and how do we go about that? If a 5-member team can reach its team goal of raising $500 in charitable sales, what can a team of 10 members do and how can we organize a larger team?

Exploring the 5 W's and the How will unleash every volunteer leader's potential to not only accomplish the goal but exceed it. Also, like a good inquisitive reporter who keeps on digging for the real story, a successful volunteer leader never gives up developing various approaches on how to accomplish their goal.

Never give up, never surrender! said Tim Allen in the 1999 movie "Galaxy Quest." Volunteer leaders . . . let your mantra also be to never give up trying new ways to accomplish your team goal. Empowering your teams to learn from failures can ultimately help them reach undisputed success.

"Where there is shouting, there is no true knowledge!"

- Leonardo da Vinci

DISCIPLINE #5:

LEAD MORE, SCREAM LESS

Attaining genuine teamwork and exceeding the goal is a thing of beauty. Reaching a milestone together as a team can be fun. It requires clarity on the objectives, focus, and discipline. Sure, everyone is cheerful when the goals are being met. But what happens if the team doesn't accomplish a goal? What is a volunteer leader to do in moments where team members are showing signs of burnout and overcommitting themselves?

Volunteer leaders who try to do everything themselves get burned out. This leads to frustration. However, volunteer leaders who exhibit professional discipline when coaching team members can help volunteers improve their performance. There will be times when the leader must apply coaching or methods of discipline to alert a team member that a behavior is potentially inhibiting team productivity. Screaming and shouting orders is not leading. Discover how to lead and not just how to go through the motions. Empower your teams to lead.

Have you ever encountered an unhappy team member shouting orders or screaming over the phone? It is not pretty, nor productive!

Years ago, while was serving in a top volunteer role, the hours spent began to take their toll on the entire team. It was becoming exhausting and difficult to be at every meeting every day for everybody. Aside from a 40-hour-a-week job, picking up kids from school, and trying to spend some time with family, much time was needed to just catch up on some emails and phone calls. It was during one of these moments when I got a call from one of my chairpersons.

"David, we need to be at ALL of these clubs!" she shouted. "I CAN'T DO THIS BY MYSELF!"

I understood her frustration and told her "Sounds like we should delegate some of these visits," explaining that other members had expressed wanting to pitch in. But, she wasn't hearing any of that, saying with a piercing tone, "THE VISITS NEED TO BE HANDLED CORRECTLY!"

By this time during the phone conversation, her voice was hitting 99% on the Richter scale! Insisting that she calm down, I asserted, "No one is expecting you to visit every early-morning or afternoon club." I explained the need to respect people for the time they can afford to visit clubs and their need to keep their jobs.

Standing in the kitchen about 15 feet away was my mom (who has since passed on). "Who in the world is that on the phone?" Mom asked, seemingly very concerned.

The screaming was so intense I had to put the phone down and walk away for a moment. When I returned to the phone moments later, the chairperson was still screaming out orders. Seems she never skipped a screaming beat. By now, it was becoming annoying and somewhat amusing. In an effort to empathize, I suggested that it would be okay to delegate this particular task to someone else. Or, better yet, step aside for a bit and take a break. Wow! That seemed to hit a nerve.

"WHAT??" she screeched. "WHY WOULD YOU SAY THAT! I'M DOING THIS FOR YOUUUU!!!!"

No one should get so over committed and frustrated that it calls for yelling at team members. It does occur though. There are and will be over-demanding leaders, some with well-deserved reputations for raising their voice. Some experts might concur that yelling could be an integral part of their leadership and management style. In fact, this behavior is the norm in some professions such as military or professional sports.

Some leadership experts have written about this type of culture. Author of the book, "The No Asshole Rule," Stanford Professor Bob Sutton expresses he is not quick to condemn leaders who raise their voices with intent. (With intent is the key concept here). "To me it is all about context and culture," he told another writer in an email, "and the history of the relationship." But in a volunteer organization? Hardly. It doesn't seem to fit the culture. I mean, ask yourself, does a person actually pay better attention to someone yelling? Wouldn't they find it demotivating?

Yelling at members is a bitter sting to a volunteer team. My mom always told me, "You can catch more bees with honey than you can with vinegar." Well, maybe a lot of our moms said the same thing. Some say more flies, but ugh, who wants those? Here's the point; volunteers will do more for leaders who are kind and less for those who are rude.

Volunteers are . . . volunteering!!! They are donating their time, for free! Any leader overseeing volunteers should talk with them with respect. Of course, there are times when volunteers need to be coached about an issue. It is far more human and effective to go about it with sensitive care. There is no need to be cynical or use hurtful tones if a team member fails to respond with urgency to a request. Learn to communicate in a nurturing, supportive, and dignified manner. Sum it up this way: you can lead a person to the water, but don't shove their face down in it!

41

Leading or Just Taking A Walk?

Leadership requires a TEAM. Sure, it's the overused acronym for Together Everyone Accomplishes More. But isn't it the truth? The best time a volunteer leader can spend is investing time to mentor, coach, and lead team members to the finish line. This, too, takes discipline. Spend time trying to become a better leader. Being better leaders helps us to become better human beings.

How can a person determine if he or she is a good or effective leader? Leadership expert John Maxwell suggests a great way to determine that. In his book "The 25 Irrefutable Laws of Leadership," he suggests joining a volunteer organization and leading a group of people is the best way for a person to determine whether they're a good leader. Maxwell humors, "If you find you're being a good leader people will follow you. That means you're leading. But, if you think you are leading a group of people but turn around and see no one is following, then you are merely taking a walk!" What a visually thoughtful way of putting it.

The following are some great attributes of successful volunteer leaders:

- Leaders know they're only as good as their team.
- Leaders have vision and show others the way.
- Great leaders lead their team by example.
- Leaders know volunteers follow people they trust.
- Successful leaders know kindness goes a long way.

Successful volunteer leaders embrace the contributions of diversified abilities. These leaders give volunteers the vision, support, and guidance to become leaders themselves. As Maxwell asserts, "It takes a leader to raise up a leader."

Accomplishing goals in a volunteer organization requires keen focus. Practice the discipline of being a servant leader at every stage of the journey. Effective leaders live to serve. They can see what others sometimes can't. They plan their work and work their plan. They celebrate their teams' successes! In other words, they have what we have coined as "VIPER Power." The term "viper" is derived from the Latin word vipera, -ae, also possibly from vivus ("living"). Disciplined and effective volunteer leaders with VIPER power are Visionary, Inspirational, and they Plan, Execute, and Recognize their teams as winners. With vision a leader can see the goal. Through insight a leader can share relevant guidance. With a plan a leader can chart a path to success. Through execution a leader can make things happen. Through recognition a leader can keep volunteers coming back.

Don't Play the Victim Role

Even leaders with VIPER power will draw their fair share of critics. As expressed by 26th U.S. President Theodore Roosevelt, "There is nothing worse than the cowardice of cynicism…. The poorest way to face life is to face it with a sneer." He continued, "There are many who confine themselves to criticism of the way others do what they themselves dare not even attempt." As a volunteer leader, avoid excuses or whining about not being able to accomplish team goals. Above all, don't complain about what other people or teams are doing, or what "can't" be done. Take accountability for the team, and its actions. Above all, don't play the victim role; it's discouraging and demotivating. Playing victim, in the urban sense of the word, means playing or pretending to be the underdog, the victim in every problem in his or her life. People who play victim are quick to point fingers at others for their own shortcomings. Finger pointing and lack of accountability can negatively impact a team's ability to achieve its mission.

In many volunteer organizations, membership is the lifeline to the business. Some years ago, a marketing director was heard constantly telling his team and colleagues, "Well, no one ever told me about doing that!" He exclaimed, "Hey,

I'm not doing all of that!" even though membership was clearly his responsibility! Statements like these are disparaging and show disrespect and contempt for the team and its efforts to reach success.

Holding a team accountable, as well as yourself as a volunteer leader takes discipline. Stay away from the victim role and excuses why something can't be done. Before holding team members accountable, volunteer leaders must hold themselves accountable. Sure, it takes discipline and practice, and is easier said than done. It pays off though. Volunteer leaders who hold themselves accountable actualize their leadership potential faster. There can be no real leadership if a volunteer leader demands excellence from others but doesn't demand excellence from him or herself.

Finally, showing appreciation for your team efforts is the icing on the cake. Show appreciation by recognizing current and past team leaders for any contributions they've made. In volunteer organizations, recognition is a volunteer's currency. Recognizing past leaders demonstrates integrity and respect whether we like them or not! Few behaviors are more disrespectful than not recognizing members and leaders for their contributions.

Outgoing leaders should also avoid solely glorifying themselves for record-breaking milestones. Always credit your team's effort ahead of yours. Why? Volunteers are not paid for their services. Recognition is their currency for achieving milestones, and one of the only currencies that will keep volunteers coming back to serve.

A SHORT STORY ON LETTING GO

One day, two monks set out for a temple in a valley beyond the woods. While cutting a pathway through the woods, they came across a choppy stream they needed to cross. There, standing by the bank of the stream, was a beautiful young maiden dressed in silk. She was clearly at a loss as to how to cross without getting muddy and wet.

Without thinking twice, the elder monk gestured to pick her up. Shocked, she obliged. He put her over his shoulder and waded across to the other side. The younger monk, dismayed and uneasy at what he had witnessed, followed in tow.

Upon reaching the other side of the bank, the elder monk put the maiden down gently. The maiden paid her respects to the monks and walked on. The monks then continued on their way to the temple.

As they navigated through the forest, the younger monk, still troubled by what he'd seen, asked;

"How could you do that? We aren't even supposed to make eye contact with women, let alone pick them up and carry them!"

Immediately, the elder monk turned to the younger monk and expressed, "Dear Brother, I put her down when I reached the other side of the stream. But you are still carrying her in your mind."

Moral of the story: Be mindful of holding on to things that have occurred in the past. Don't allow the past to prevent you, as a volunteer or volunteer leader, from moving forward.

"Anything that you have to control, controls you"

- Guy Finley

DISCIPLINE #6:

LET GO OF THAT MONKEY!

There's another universal truth about leadership: a leader must learn to delegate! One person cannot do it all. Volunteer leaders who find undisputed success are those who learn to let go and let the team succeed.

The Monkey Trap

Volunteer leaders grow by disciplining themselves to learn how to let go and empower others. There is a valuable lesson in this story about the Monkey Trap:

In certain indigenous cultures, the natives use a heavily weighted gourd or similar object to trap monkeys. They drill a hole in it just large enough for a monkey's hand to pass through, insert some nuts or fruit inside, and place the gourd where a monkey will find it. When a monkey approaches the gourd, the monkey sticks its hand through the hole and clutches the food. But with the food clenched in its grasp, the monkey can't get its hand back out. Its fist is balled up and the hole is too small for its hand to pass through. The gourd is too heavy for the monkey to carry. Because the monkey will not let go of its prize, it becomes trapped and gives up its freedom for a small piece of food. It seems obvious that all the monkey needs to do is unclench its hand, let go of the bait, and escape. But because it views the treat as its possession and is not willing to let go, the monkey is trapped and loses its freedom.

Volunteer leaders can encounter the same behavior of enabling. It's the "monkey mentality," a colloquial term for doing other people's work. Heck, we may even be one of the monkeys ourselves! Yes, our goal is to help others become empowered and to succeed. But there is a difference between "helping" and "enabling." Leaders who don't recognize this soon get overwhelmed. Here's a conversation shared by a director colleague who experienced this with his team:

> *"Deep down, I recognized some team members were stuck on old ideas. I found myself letting them do it their way. Even worse, I then started doing the work for them, just to keep things moving. Next thing I knew, I started carrying their load, too. Now, I was not only struggling to accomplish my own tasks, but I started carrying the weight of five other team members' jobs! It seemed like I had started carrying their monkeys!"*

Some volunteer leaders are innately people pleasers; leaders considered extremely helpful to everyone and who never say no. We spend a vast amount of time doing things for everyone possible. We start carrying the monkey for several team members. Let's recognize one thing. People come with baggage. But, to accomplish the team goal, everyone must do his or her part. What does that mean? It means you need to stop carrying people's baggage for them and get their monkey off your back. Let go and give it back to them. Empower the team members to get the job done. Allow the team to experience the journey of resolving issues and conflicts and creating solutions to reach their goal.

What's more, it is beneficial to understand the detriment of holding on to team members, ideas, and behaviors that don't serve the team. Being attached to detrimental concepts and unaccountable team members restricts the team from the freedom to accomplish the goal.

Making the decision to control team members, holding on to selfish ideas, or empowering them by letting go is simply a matter of making a choice. Without a doubt, leading and managing people, projects, and goals can be a challenge. A volunteer leader who has a desire to achieve undisputed success must discipline his or herself to make these choices regularly. Think of the word "CHOICE" as the acronym for CHoosing to Overcome Incredible Challenges Every day.

More than a decade ago, Sam, a really close friend (more like a brother), shared his thoughts on why leaders have such a difficult time choosing to do the right thing. Sam is a jack-of-all-trades kind of guy; professional chef, musician, gardener, I.T. computer expert, trainer; you name it, Sam can do it.

"I wonder why some of us as leaders, or people for that matter, experience so much challenge in their lives," Sam pondered, while we were adjourning a management training session. "My thinking is that it's because of the selfish choices they make in life," he exclaimed. "It seems clear that if we make better choices in life, we would be better people."

The conversation that day stuck to me for years to come. As a matter of fact, Sam humored me one year with a small gift to commemorate my successfully completing one year as a volunteer leader. It was a large, white, 12-oz coffee mug. On it was a quote written in a large black font:

"The Difficulty in Life Is the Choice."

Serving as a leader in a volunteer organization can give us a wonderful opportunity to practice making good choices. And through the practice of making good choices, we become better people. We then begin to emulate the characteristics of a good leader, a good human being. Making good choices can lead to greater productivity or just more fun in life. Either way, the choices we make, whether good or bad, begin to shape our thoughts and our actions. Perhaps this is the reason why some volunteers who work in addiction recovery volunteer organizations say;

"You make the choice, and then the choice makes you."

Serving as a volunteer leader can be a joy. It's much more fun when we make the choice to let the creative processes take place organically. Take time to balance family, work, and volunteering. Have some fun working in unison with your team. Your team members should have some fun and a life, and so should you! Make volunteering a rewarding, fulfilling, and fun experience. A team that plays together stays together! Balance is the key here.

How do we find the time to do all the stuff we need to do? How do we balance our time and energy between our home, our family, our regular job, and our personal goals?

Everything is about balance. Balancing life is important. It plays a vital role in accomplishing goals as a leader. It protects us from being overburdened with stress.

There are some proven methods we can use to achieve balance. Communicate the hours you're available during the week. Utilize technology such as email or text messaging to get updates. Turn off your cell phone at certain times to give you time to handle personal matters. Learn when to say "no" and avoid committing to projects out of guilt. We can't be everywhere for everybody every time we are asked. Guard your private and/or family time. Every leader can benefit from having some personal time for reflection or just to "smell the roses."

My friends, we can learn to live and laugh more if we learn to just let go. No one describes this perspective better than the late comedian George Carlin. He often joked about the funny paradoxes of life. He put it all in perspective in one of the more serious reflections he wrote after the World Trade Center tragedy on 9-11-2001. To paraphrase the story, he wrote:

"The paradox of our time in history is that we have taller buildings but shorter tempers ...we spend more but have less....we have more experts yet more problems...more medicine but less wellness...we have learned to make a living but not a life...these are days of two-income families but more divorce...we should spend time with our loved ones because they won't be around forever, and give time to share the precious thoughts in our mind...because life is not measured by the number of breaths we take, but by the moments that take our breath away."

Let's learn to let go.

"Everything you want in life has a price connected to it. There's a price to pay if you want to make things better, a price to pay just for leaving things as they are, a price for everything."

−Harry Browne

DISCIPLINE #7:

NO SACRIFICE, NO SUCCESS

What's the adage? There is a price to pay for everything. Nothing could be closer to truth. Ever ask someone to volunteer for a project and there was an extraordinary long pause before they open their mouth to answer? You can bet he or she was thinking, "What is this going to cost me?" Sometimes this comes to mind even before they ask, "what's in it for me?" What is the price for volunteering or leading a team of volunteers? Let's take a look:

Time: We spend long hours in team meetings, on the phone, reading and writing emails, and texting. We sacrifice time from work, family, and our personal matters.

Money: Volunteer organizations operate on budgets developed to reimburse volunteers. Reimbursement is the magic word. The rule of thumb is "spend first, then reimburse!"

Relationships: Who can we call on to help us with our task? Or should I say, who won't run the opposite way when we ask them to volunteer? Some volunteers who are constantly approached are burned out from volunteering.

If these are the costs, what are some potential "cost saving" tips to consider? How about these:

Time: Plan each day, hour by hour, the day before. Schedule early-morning team meetings over the phone. Stop spending time hunting down a meeting room. It's convenient for most and can save a lot of time.

Money: Develop a personal volunteer budget for everything. Do your research and determine how much you are willing to spend on items. Most, if not all, volunteer organizations have a budget. Plan events well ahead of time and submit a requisition for funds.

Relationships: It's all about relationship power. If a member won't commit to a task for you, find out who else they would do it for. Work through relationships to get your goals accomplished.

> **"If you don't sacrifice for what you want,
> then what you want becomes the sacrifice"**
> - Anonymous

Without sacrifices, success becomes a bit difficult to achieve. To get something, something has to give. There have to be some sacrifices. Take baseball, for instance. With a man on third base and no outs, a batter will risk hitting a "fly ball" that can easily be caught if it means allowing a runner to steal home plate and score.

Volunteer leaders who sacrifice time to help others will find others who will sacrifice their time to help them. Think of it like your bank account when you visit your local ATM machine. If you don't deposit money in the account, you certainly can't withdraw money from the account. Nothing in, nothing out! As the leader, we must make deposits.

Think about some scenarios you may have encountered. The finance manager won't cut a check early to pay for a venue. The PR person won't take the extra time to design and make changes to the promo fliers. Team members won't show up on time to the events. Why? Well, when did you last take time to discover that the people you count on have other commitments as well? Unless you've deposited some of your personal time to get to know people, they won't give you the time you need from them. We can't always take, take, take.

Try this analogy on for size. Are you a person who spends more time wanting to be fed rather than spending time serving others? Sometimes, we must stop worrying about being fed all the time. We have to learn to take off the bib and put on our apron to start serving others. We have to start giving in order to start receiving.

Here is another analogy that illustrates this point. It is about two bodies of water, sharing the same region, the same source of water. Yet one sea is full of life, while the other is dead.

The river Jordan flows into and through the Sea of Galilee, and then flows out towards the Dead Sea. The water simply passes through; which keeps the Sea of Galilee healthy, vibrant, and teeming with marine life. But the Dead Sea is so far below average sea level that it has no outlet. The water flows in from the river Jordan but does not flow out. It is estimated that over a million tons of water evaporate from the Dead Sea every day; leaving it salty, full of minerals, and unfit for any marine life. Everything dies in the Dead Sea. The Sea of Galilee takes and gives, yet the Dead Sea only takes.

When a volunteer leader begins to discipline him or herself to help others, a life-changing revelation occurs. It's not always about the leader! Ever encounter a leader who takes all the credit? Maybe you encountered one who favors decisions that only benefit the leader's personal motive. Or one who modifies the plan to accommodate that one and only person who does not like it. Now, I am not a big fan of the Star Trek movie series, but there is truth in the suggestion Captain Spock gives to his friend Captain Kirk. Spock repeatedly reminds Jim Kirk, "The needs of the few should not outweigh the needs of the many."

In a Forbes article, contributor Joseph Folkman conducted a

Zenger-Folkman assessment gathered from over 3,800 leaders. It measured their effectiveness using a 360-degree evaluation process taken by managers, peers, direct reports, and others. Each person was assessed on their tendency to take or give credit to others. The study revealed that leaders whose tendency was to take credit were rated as ineffective leaders (13th percentile). The study showed leaders who give credit to others were rated as some of the most effective leaders (85th percentile).

At the end of the day, a good leader wants to ensure that his or her volunteers "live to volunteer another day!" Sacrifices come with the territory of success. It's important to understand what sacrifices to make. Often, by panicking to accomplish a goal at the last minute, a volunteer leader may push their team members to the brink of quitting. The leader will tell themselves, "If I can sacrifice my personal and family time, so can they!" Well, be careful, my fellow volunteer leaders. Human emotion is the driving force of serving as a volunteer in the first place. An effective volunteer leader benefits better by igniting their team members to carry the torch and get the task accomplished. Pushing the right team members the wrong way can cause a mutiny. It is best to know when and how much to push your team members. Knowing how to push your team takes discipline and patience. It takes what we call "kindling leadership."

Kindling Leadership

Teams need encouragement to keep their flame of enthusiasm ablaze. This prevents them from feeling as though they have failed. As Senior Patrol Leaders in the Boy Scouts of America, we learned to create campfires using nothing but sticks and twigs as kindling. Once we got a spark to ignite a little ember, we learned to blow just hard enough to keep the twigs glowing red, waiting for a small flame to arise.

NO SACRIFICE, NO SUCCESS

If we didn't blow hard enough or we blew too hard, the fire would extinguish. The same concept applies to recruiting or encouraging volunteers to work harder. Push too much and you push them away not enough and they won't grow or accomplish the goal. Sometimes it takes more than just support and encouragement. A good volunteer leader learns to push their teams just a bit, as necessary, and hold them accountable. There are times you have to push your team members.

A longtime friend, Curtis, shared a humorous tale about what I call "The Push." He heard the story from another longtime friend (who heard it from another longtime friend, and so on, and so on). He would tell this story about a billionaire who threw a grand, magnificent party at his monstrous mansion.

At the mansion was this enormous, art deco styled swimming pool. Inside the pool were active, swimming alligators! As a humorous gesture, the billionaire offered to grant a world of wealth to anyone brave enough to swim the length of the alligator-filled pool. The crowd of 100 or so guests began to chuckle with amusement. Right at that moment, the guests heard a loud splash. In the pool, they saw a young man swimming fiercely for his life, escaping the snaps of each of those alligators. Remarkably, the young man swam from one end of the pool to the other end, and with great urgency, leaped right out.

The billionaire and guests gasped in astonishment. The billionaire was amazed and speechless. "I was merely joking," the billionaire chuckled, "I didn't think anyone would actually do it." As he promised the billionaire offered the young man his choice of wealth; money, gold, or whatever he wanted. The young man looked bewildered and was out of breath. He took a long gasp for air and screamed loudly, "I only want one thing...the name of the (freakin') person who pushed me into the pool!"

The moral of the story? Sometimes it takes an ordinary push to motivate people to accomplish extraordinary things.

57

"Discipline is the bridge between goals and accomplishments."

\- Entrepreneur Jim Rohn

TYING IT ALL TOGETHER

Looking to find your purpose? Get involved in volunteer leadership. It can provide a true revelation on how to become the leader that, deep down inside, you know you can be. Becoming an effective volunteer leader means becoming a disciplined leader. Being a disciplined leader requires knowing your team, knowing who they are and what motivates them. Know their lives, their families, and their interests. A volunteer leader can never become more important than the members or the mission of the team.

Discover your own leadership disciplines and your own truths. Know that people want to be part of a winning team. Leading in a volunteer organization can help you find your why. And when you find your why, you find success. Stay focused on your mission and learn to embrace your failures. Doing so can create inspiring opportunities to be a successful volunteer leader. Serving as a volunteer leader can create the right platform for learning how to avoid "enabling" your team members; do for them what they can do for themselves..

Enabling your team members can prevents them from learning, demonstrating independence, and can hinder the creative decision making process. Empower and encourage your team members to take ownership of the team goal, Effective leaders help their teams to foster a commitment to accomplishing the team goal. Help your team members become more accountable. Let go and let the process of learning take place. Above all, where there is no sacrifice, there can be no success. Sacrifice requires discipline, and discipline can lead to undisputed success.

5 BEST PRACTICES OF LEADERSHIP

Among the many books and articles on leadership lies a great number of helpful insights and techniques. Every volunteer leader has an opinion on what works and what doesn't. If the true intention is to become an effective volunteer leader, do some homework. Search for techniques that seem to be universal with achieving success.

There are hundreds of goal-accomplishing techniques. Below are five (5) practices that can catapult the success level of any team.

Practice #1:

What Gets Measured, Gets Done

As a volunteer leader, we could spend countless hours planning and meeting but fail to accomplish a set goal. Volunteer leaders sometimes find themselves doing "busy" work" rather than doing "productive work." Doing "busy work is performing an activity with no results. Doing productive work is performing an activity that gains positive results. How can you tell the difference? By setting a goal and documenting (measuring) the results. Chances are, if the goal doesn't get measured the goal doesn't get done.

Consistent measuring and reporting keeps a leader focused. We call these measurements Key Performance Indicators (KPI's). These KPI's help us make relevant decisions and achieve results. They reflect your team or organization's critical success goals. They provide a snapshot of where you and your team are at all times. The key is to measure that which is relevant to the task at hand.

In a customer service environment, key indicators can point out how long customers are on hold. If a manager sees high "hold times," it could mean representatives are spending too much time resolving customer issues. For a volunteer team raising ad revenue, KPI's could help determine the number of ads secured in a specific time frame. For example, your 5-member ad team's goal can be to sell 60 ads in a 5-week period. In this case, to hit the goal, the team will need to sell 12 ads per week. The KPI for each team member would be 2-3 ads each week.

The important rule is to ensure to measure what is important and relevant. Take it from Albert Einstein, "Not everything that counts can be counted, and not everything that can be counted counts." Sure, it's a numbers game. But, we gamble away our chances for success when we don't track the numbers. Volunteer leaders can guarantee success when they measure specific performances because what gets measured gets done.

Practice #2:

Define Your Moment: Make A Decision

Consider this scene: a chairperson and her team are discussing the final phases of organizing a quarterly recognition event. They are agonizing over a decision. The organization has budgeted for six awardees to be recognized for the 2nd quarter. Awards have been purchased, the venue has been paid for, and guests have been notified. The problem is, four awardees cannot attend the ceremony.

The committee faces a tough decision: do they cancel the event and wait for the next quarter, or move on with the ceremony for only two people because everything is set to go? The chairperson fears the decision she makes will shape her legacy in this position.

Any volunteer serving in a leadership role will always face a defining moment and tough decisions. Should they take the easy way out or make the tough decision?

Focusing so much on making the "right" decision can inevitably lead to leadership paralysis. It is not always easy to know the best decision. What's the best way to handle it? Embrace the defining moment and make a decision. Keep a few things in mind:

1. Be clear on the purpose and the stakeholders. Will the action be in alignment with the organization's or the members' welfare?
2. Don't focus on the immediate impact of the situation, but rather the bigger picture. Evaluate the benefits and consequences.
3. Expect that someone is not going to like the decision no matter what. Volunteer leaders will always be faced with a moment of truth. Again, focusing on your leadership and organization's values will help provide direction.
4. Get feedback from past leaders. Open your feedback channel to those who have served before as well as trusted advisors. Defining moments may help create a legacy of true Servant Leadership. No matter the option chosen, the support achieved may be more important than the final decision itself.
5. Make the decision and move on!

Take it from the character Tim McAvoy in the movie "Tin Cup," "When a defining moment comes along, either you define the moment or the moment defines you."

Practice #3:
Always K.I.S.S.

Here is an idea for the ages. On every leadership decision and project, successful volunteer leaders always KISS! That's right, they Keep It Simple & Straightforward. Now of course, some say, "keep it simple stupid." But no one should be considered stupid for keeping anything simple. Experience shows, keeping decisions and tasks simple achieves results. Processes that are simple to understand make great transition plans for leaders next in command. Active volunteer leaders can learn a lot from the words of activist and journalist Martin Rubin, "Life is simple. You just have to stop trying to figure it out."

Practice #4:
Failing to Plan is Planning to Fail

Ben Franklin was quoted as saying, "*Failing to plan is planning to fail.*" One of the greatest obstacles volunteer leaders face is actually putting together a plan that works. Planning helps volunteer leaders stay focused on what's important. Planning keeps a leader and the team from trying to figure it out. Volunteer leaders who don't plan get caught up in other people's demands and plans. Planning helps minimize risk and makes tough decisions easier. Planning makes the volunteer experience a worthy one for those who donate their time. It enables teams to see the short-range tasks, which helps to accomplish the mid-range tasks, which helps to accomplish the long-range tasks and ultimately the bottom line. Having a plan means that everyone can be on the same page.

Some may ask, why not just do what Nike says and "Just Do It?" The question becomes, what is the "it" you're talking about. From years of mentoring, coaching, and chairing hundreds of activities and events, having no plan at all can be the first sign of failure waiting to happen. Lack of planning leads to volunteers making complaints like these:

- "We didn't have the right people for the job."
- "It was unrealistic for us to hit that goal."
- "People volunteered but they never showed up to the meetings."
- "So many of us had no idea what needed to be done."

Therefore, where there is no plan, there is no successful accomplishment.

Practice #5:

It's Always Possible to Achieve the Impossible

"Start by doing what's necessary; then do what's possible; and suddenly you are doing the impossible," - Saint Francis of Assisi.

As a district leader in Toastmasters International, starting new clubs is one of the "critical success factors." Critical success factors are those elements that must be accomplished in order for a district to reach the level of becoming "Distinguished." Reaching Distinguished indicates and measures the success level of all clubs, areas, divisions, and districts. Newly elected Club Growth district leaders are responsible for launching/chartering these new clubs. Marketing (Club Growth) teams charter more than 1,000 new Toastmasters clubs each year, according one edition of the "How To Build a Toastmasters Club" guide. With 100+ districts worldwide, that averages out to be just about 10 new clubs in each district, every year.

In North America regions, some districts may struggle to consistently hit their new club goal. Often, a new club growth director will complain how impossible it is to start 15+ clubs in a district already saturated with existing clubs. Not so though. One year, District 1 Toastmasters in southern California chartered over 25 clubs, and surpassed that success a few years later with 31 clubs! How was that so? By simply focusing on what could be done instead of complaining about what couldn't be done. Of course the next complaint was "not all of those clubs were 'real' clubs!" Well, who can be the judge of that? Bottom line, the leaders did what was necessary, without screaming at each other. Leaders who have fun working together are those who stick to a plan. They keep club chartering processes simple. They empower team members and avoid micro-managing. It is very possible your team could perform some impossible feats by sticking to the necessities of what needs to be done.

5 BEST PRACTICES OF COMMUNICATION

Communication is a two-way mechanism. Volunteer leaders send and receive a barrage of information every minute of every day. Sometimes volunteers want answers to their questions and concerns right away. Information travels so quickly through social media, phone calls, emails, and texts. Some responses require the opinion(s) of more than just one leader. In these cases, here are five (5) best practices to attain effective communication in a media driven environment:

Communication Overflow (It's A Good Thing)
1. It's better to over communicate than to not communicate enough. Follow-up is the key to effectiveness. If you receive no reply in 1-2 days, follow up using a different mode of communication.
2. Different leaders hear/receive information in different ways. Try different approaches: personal notes, brief meetings, email, or social media. "Dumb down" the message to ensure it's understood.
3. Utilize email and social media etiquette. If two or more people receive the same message, review it and decide who should respond. Confer with each person on who needs to respond. Support the decision of the responder. Above all, don't cc everyone.
4. Be mindful when responding to angry email. Review with objectivity; don't respond out of anger. Wait a few hours to respond. Ask for clarification if needed.
5. Avoid writing an email out of anger. If you find yourself doing so, don't send it right away. Wait an hour or two and review the email. Waiting can help you discover a more effective way of getting your message across.

VOLUNTEER BILL OF RIGHTS

&

VOLUNTEER LEADER RESPONSIBILITIES

BILL OF RIGHTS

Every volunteer has rights, and every volunteer leader has responsibilities. These lists were created from an assortment of resources and personal leadership experiences. To achieve fair and maximum results, it is fair to say that all volunteers have rights and all volunteer leaders have responsibilities.

Volunteer Bill of Rights

1. The Right to feel valued and be heard
2. The Right to choose how you volunteer
3. The Right to say No or to leave
4. The Right to open and transparent communication
5. The Right to be supported and feel safe
6. The Right to have and know information about your role and/or your chosen project
7. The Right to be treated with respect and kindness
8. The Right to be given a task that fits your values, background, and experience
9. The Right to receive proper guidance, direction, and training to achieve goals
10. The Right to be recognized and appreciated

VOLUNTEER LEADER
RESPONSIBILITIES
(Modified to adequately fit the needs of any leader)

Volunteer leaders bear some responsibility to ensure that volunteers are being supported and guided properly:

Volunteer Leader Responsibilities

1. The Responsibility to conduct meetings to keep team(s) informed
2. The Responsibility to start and end meetings on time
3. The Responsibility to always have an agenda for each meeting
4. The Responsibility to guide, manage, and approve proposed changes to keep agenda on track
5. The Responsibility to know what's going on with the team
6. The Responsibility to understand the meaning of every idea and/or proposed action
7. The Responsibility to have all facts, alternatives, and consequences presented and discussed before making final decisions
8. The Responsibility to effectively select, train, and guide officers and leaders who chair committees
9. The Responsibility to make timely changes to the team to achieve overall success
10. The Responsibility to make information available to team members or officers, except in matters that may hurt or harm them or another person

FIND YOUR ORGANIZATION

VOLUNTEER ORGANIZATIONS

Serving as a volunteer or a volunteer leader can be ever so rewarding and life-changing. Finding the right role in the right organization for the right reason can help any person find his or her purpose in life. Here is a partial list of organizations you can serve as a volunteer or a volunteer leader:

Advocacy Groups for Human Rights and Civil Liberties
Charities that help people fight for rights through legal advocacy or education, awareness, and funding for human rights initiatives.

American Civil Liberties Union
American Jewish World Service
Americans United
Amnesty International
Anti-Defamation League
Association on American Indian Affairs
Children's Defense Fund
Coalition to Stop Gun Violence
The Carter Center
Center for Constitutional Rights
Committee for Missing Children
Doctors of the World
FreedomtoChoose Project
Human Rights Watch
NAACP
The Center for Victims of Torture
Committee to Protect Journalists
Center for Community Change
Victims of Crime
United Way
Peace Corp

LIST OF ORGANIZATIONS (Con't)

Animal Rights
Animal rights organizations that seek to protect animals and their habitats through advocacy and action-based and educational initiatives.

African Wildlife Foundation
American Humane Association
American Assoc. for the Prevention of Cruelty to Animals
Animal Legal Defense Fund
Animal Welfare Institute
Best Friends Animal Society
Born Free USA
Defenders of Wildlife
Doris Day Animal League
D.E.L.T.A. Rescue
Dian Fossey Gorilla Fund International
The Elephant Sanctuary in Tennessee
Farm Sanctuary
Friends of Animals
Humane Farming Association
Humane Society of the United States
Marine Mammal Center
National Audubon Society
Performing Animal Welfare Society (P.A.W.S.)
Pet Partners
RedRover
Wildlife Conservation Society

LIST OF ORGANIZATIONS (Con't)

Land Conservation and the Environment

Charities that seek to protect the environment through education, research, action, political, legal advocacy and conservation initiatives.

American Farmland Trust
American Forests
American Rivers
Appalachian Trail Conservancy
Beyond Pesticides
Blue Ocean Institute
Carbon Fund
Center for Biological Diversity
Chesapeake Bay Foundation
Coral Reef Alliance
Cousteau Society
Earth Island Institute
Earthjustice
Environmental Defense Fund
Farm Aid
Greenpeace
Keep America Beautiful
National Park Foundation
Ocean Conservancy

General Emergency Relief

These organizations step in and provide relief during difficult times such as natural disaster and war.

American Red Cross
Children's Disaster Services
Emergency Nutrition Network
Firefighters' Charitable Foundation

LIST OF ORGANIZATIONS (Con't)

Refugees

Organizations that provide support for people forced to flee their homeland due to war, famine, political unrest, disease, and natural disaster.

Africa and Middle East Refugee Assistance
American Near East Refugee Aid
American Refugee Committee
International Rescue Committee

Medical Assistance

Programs that provide medical & emergency relief and assistance to people who may not otherwise have access to affordable care for financial, social, or geographical reasons.

AmeriCares
Catholic Medical Missions Board
CURE International
Direct Relief International
Doctors Without Borders
International Medical Corps
Medical Teams International
Operation Smile
Samaritan's Purse
World Medical Relief

LIST OF ORGANIZATIONS (Con't)

Education, Leadership Research & Cultural Preservation Groups

Groups with missions geared towards improving education, providing more educational opportunities, promoting cultural awareness, or preserving the culture of specific populations.

ACCESS College Foundation
Africa-America Institute
AFS USA
American Enterprise Institute
American Indian College Fund
Asia Society
Building Educated Leaders for Life (BELL)
Hispanic Scholarship Fund
Scholarship America
Toastmasters International

Health: Research, and Education

Foundations that focus on research about specific illnesses. Many also have an educational component to enlighten people about prevention and management strategies.

AIDS Research Alliance
Alliance for Aging Research
American Heart Association
American Stroke Association
Arthritis Research Institute of America
Avon Foundation
Breast Cancer Research Foundation
City of Hope/Beckman Research Institute
Epilepsy Foundation
ALS Association

LIST OF ORGANIZATIONS (Con't)

American Diabetes Association
Autism Speaks
Hearing Health Foundation
Juvenile Diabetes Research Foundation
Lupus Research Institute
Brain and Behavior Research Foundation
First Candle
March of Dimes

Support for Chronic Illnesses and Diseases

These organizations provide financial, emotional, or medical support for people with chronic illnesses and their loved one.

Alzheimer's Association
American Kidney Fund
American Leprosy Missions
American Liver Foundation
American Lung Association
American Parkinson Disease Association
Arthritis Foundation
Bailey House
CaringBridge
Cystic Fibrosis Foundation
Easter Seals
Huntington's Disease Society of America
Project Sunshine
The Sunshine Kids

LIST OF ORGANIZATIONS (Con't)

Cancer Support and Research
Cancer charities that provide research and support for people with cancer and their loved ones; may include education and emotional support.

American Brain Tumor Association
American Cancer Society
Breast Cancer
Cancer and Careers
CancerCare
Cancer Federation
Cancer Fund of America
Cancer Recovery Foundation
Cancer Research Institute
St Jude's Children's Research Hospital
Children's Cancer and Blood Foundation
National Children's Cancer Society
Children's Cancer Research Fund
Jimmy Fund
Dana-Farber Cancer Institute
Livestrong

Support for Physical and Cognitive Disabilities
These charities provide financial support, education, and research for people with physical and mental disabilities, as well as their families.

Achilles International
American Action Fund for Blind Children and Adults
American Association of the Deaf-Blind
American Foundation for Disabled Children
Christopher and Dana Reeve Foundation
Heritage for the Blind
The ARC
United Spinal Association

LIST OF ORGANIZATIONS (Con't)

Poverty
These organizations help the economically disadvantaged around the world with an array of programs such as education, advocacy, health care, housing, and anti-hunger programs.

Catholic Charities USA
Catholic Relief Services
Christian Appalachian Project
Christian Relief Services
Coalition for the Homeless
Lutheran World Relief
Modest Needs

Feeding the Hungry
These charities fight hunger around the world by providing food, clean water, and funding.

Action Against Hunger
Africare
Bread for the World
Care
City Harvest
Farmers and Hunters Feeding the Hungry
Feeding America
Feed My People
Food Bank for New York City
Society of St. Andrew

Promoting Self Sufficiency
These charities help people help themselves through education, micro loans, and similar initiatives.

Accion International
Agros International

LIST OF ORGANIZATIONS (Con't)

National Relief Charities
Bowery Residents' Committee
Brother's Brother Foundation
Center for Community Change
Dress for Success
FINCA International
Food for the Hungry
Habitat for Humanity
Heifer International
Wings of Hope

Impoverished Children
These charities help children around the world who live in poverty by providing food, medicine, and education.

All God's Children
Cambodian Children's Fund
Children's Hunger Fund
World Villages for Children
Children International
ChildFund International
Compassion International
Covenant House

Senior Citizens
These charities provide advocacy, education, and research for senior citizens.
AARP Foundation
Bright Focus Foundation
National Council on Aging
OASIS Institute
Seniors Coalition

LIST OF ORGANIZATIONS (Con't)

Supporting Military and Veterans
These charities provide support services for those who serve our country, as well as their families. Services may include financial assistance, mental health care, and veterans services.

Adopt a Platoon
Air Force Aid Society
AMVETS National Service Foundation
Armed Services YMCA
Army Emergency Relief
Blinded Veterans Association
Canine Companions for Independence
Disabled American Veterans Charitable Service Trust
Paralyzed Veterans of America

Supporting Firefighters and Police
These organizations provide advocacy and support for the civil servants who keep us safe.
American Association of State Troopers
American Federation of Police and Concerned Citizens
Association for Firefighters and Paramedics
Law Enforcement Legal Defense Fund
National Fallen Firefighters Foundation
National Law Enforcement Officers Memorial Fund

Watchdog Groups

These organizations make sure public organizations like the government and the media are operating appropriately and with honesty and integrity.
Accuracy in Media
Center for Effective Government
Center for Responsive Politics

LIST OF ORGANIZATIONS (Con't)

Citizens Against Government Waste
Common Cause
Government Accountability Project
Judicial Watch
Media Research

Children and Youth
These charities support youth in a variety of ways, from providing constructive youth activities to advocating for children's rights.

Big Brothers Big Sisters of America
Boy Scouts of America
Boys and Girls Clubs of America
Campfire USA
Cedars Homes for Children
Child Find of America
Child Welfare League of America
Girl Scouts
Junior Achievement
KaBoom!
Moyer Foundation
National 4-H Council
National Center for Missing and Exploited Children
SADD

Women
Women around the world face unique issues such as discrimination, domestic violence, and human trafficking. These charities support various women's initiatives.

Catalyst
Equality Now
Family Care International
Global Fund for Women

LIST OF ORGANIZATIONS (Con't)

International Planned Parenthood Federation
League of Women Voters
National Organization for Women
National Network to End Domestic Violence
Women Employed
Soroptimist International

Prison Reform and Crime Victims Advocacy
Compassionate education and activism for incarcerated persons, their family member and other impacted by incarceration and/or crime.

Incarcerated Persons Re-Entry Support
Freedom to Choose Project
L.A. Regional Reentry Partnership
California Reentry Council Network
Insight Prison Project
Victim Support Services
National Center for Victims of Crime

APPENDIX

APPENDIX

(An abridged version of the story behind first realizing my ability to influence others. This story is depicted in "Book-To-Speeches; Stories by the Rough Writers" - 2016.)

How I Learned To Build A Bridge!

(By David Kitchen)

I often reflect upon a time in my life when I may have realized my influential leadership potential. As a kid living in Chicago, Illinois, one of my main hopes was to help build a bridge for my mom to accept a new style, a new look, a new idea. It now seems there was a defining moment that served as a bridge for me to become a leader. Our mom, Marilyn Lattimore Kitchen, was a short, slim, very fair-skinned redhead with an often boisterous personality. She loved life and was a fighter if I ever knew one. I was a middle child and often the bridge between my mom and brothers when they didn't see eye to eye on things.

She raised us like she was raised: "Kids should be seen and not heard!" She was a Keypunch Operator by profession. And the industry was primarily dominated by smart, fast-typing, professionally-dressed women. Mom was always respectable and conservative and always, *always* wore business dresses. But I remember one day seeing one of my friends' moms wearing a two-piece pant suit! A working mom wearing pants! My intentions were to persuade my mom to wear that new style and embrace a new look.

I remember talking day and night about how new moms are coming into their own wearing the new pant suit look. Of course, she was not hearing it. I have always had a gift for persuading friends and family, and my mom used to tell me, "David, you always seem to see the good in everything…" But I felt that if that was true, then she would have given in and bought a pant suit!

And then, one day, there we were: me, Lee, and Mom in Downtown Chicago, standing in a Marshall Field Store, looking for a new outfit. Then it happened. She tried on a few pant suits. "Come on, Mom," I remember uttering, "they look really nice on you." Before I knew it, seeming to like the blue and beige outfit; she smiled, draped it on her right arm, and headed for the cash register! After that day, the images of my mom wearing only dresses faded away and my new, up to-date, career-driven, keypunch-operator mom broke out of her shell. I felt that if I could influence my mom, I could influence anyone.

Perhaps that was the defining time I learned my purpose in life was to help build bridges for people so they could believe in themselves and their gifts. Today, I see my purpose in helping people build a bridge to help them envision new possibilities. And I now truly believe it all started with mom, Marilyn Lattimore Kitchen.

Point of the Story: Each of us has had a dream or a leadership experience. For many volunteer leaders, this is why volunteering and leading appears to be our calling. Take a moment to reflect on your first leadership adventure. Ponder any moment that looked like a failure but turned out to be a success in disguise. Put into action the seven disciplines outlined in this book. Perhaps it will help you find *your* why. Challenge yourself to overcome your own barriers to success by helping others to find success.

GLOSSARY OF TERMS

Distinguished Toastmaster - an award that represents the highest level of educational achievement in Toastmasters. The DTM recognizes a superior level of achievement in both communication and leadership.

Learning Orientation - the process of acquiring new, or modifying existing, knowledge, behaviors, values or skills possessed and used as a motivation variable for understanding organizational culture and/or performance.

Oxytocin - normally produced by the paraventricular nucleus of the hypothalamus and can play a role in social bonding.

Volunteer - an altruistic activity where an individual or group provides services for no financial or social gain "to benefit another person, group or organization.

Volunteer Leader - a person who leads a team or group of volunteers and provides leadership on projects and issues relating to volunteerism.

Servant Leadership - a leadership philosophy; sharing power, putting the needs of others first and helping people develop and perform as highly as possible.

Voluntold- a slang definition for describing when someone "volunteers" someone else for a task, without giving the other person a choice to say yes or no.

WIIFM - an acronym for "What's In It For Me."

REFERENCE LIST

Jenkinson et al. (2013) *Is Volunteering a Public Health Intervention?* Retrieved from URL: https://bmcpublichealth.biomedcentral.com/ articles/10.1186/1471-2458-13-773

Cameron et al. (2017) *Speeches To Books; True Stories by the Rough Writers,* Akron, OH, 48HRBOOKS

Chancellor, John (2012) *Teach The Soul,* Retrieved from URL: http://www.teachthesoul.com/2012/02/the-monkey-trap

Folksman, Joseph, (2017) *Forbes.* Retrieved from URL: https://www.forbes.com/sites/joefolkman/2017/11/10/its-all-about-me-what-happens-when-a-leader-takes-all-the-credit/#312eda3831

Frazier, Karen, (2016), *Lovetoknow,* Retrieved from URL: http://charity.lovetoknow.com/List_of_Nonprofit_Organizations

Herbers, Angie, (2015) , ThinkAdvisor. Retrieved from URL: https://www.thinkadvisor.com/2015/03/02/stay-in-your-lane

Jenette Nagy, Bill Berkowitz, Eric Wadud (2018), Community Tool Box. Retrieved from URL: https://ctb.ku.edu/en/table-of-contents/structure/volunteers/orientation-programs/main

Kanaat, Robert, (2018) *Wanderlust Worker.* Retrieved from URL: https://www.wanderlustworker.com/48-famous-failures-who-will-inspire-you-to-achieve

Leipper, Brian (2018) *The Dear Association Leader,* Engergize, Inc, Retreived from URL: (https://www.energizeinc.com/art/bill-rights-members

Lewis, Rona (2018) PlayMore Corporate Wellbeing, Los Angeles, CA Retrieved at URL: www.PlayMoreCW.com

Matthew McKay, Martha Davis, Patrick Fanning (2009), *Messages: The Communication Skills*, Oakland, CA, Harbinger

Moral Stories (2017). *We're All Just Cracked Pots*. Retrieved from URL: https://www.moralstories.org/the-cracked-pot

Maxwell, John C.,(2007), *"The 25 Irrefutable Laws of Leadership"*, Nashville, TN, Thomas Nelson Publishers

Muth, Jon J., (2006), *"Zen Shorts"*, Chicago, IL, Scholastic Press

Quote Investigator, (2014). Retrieve from URL: https://www.quoteinvestigator.com/2014/04/06/they-feel

r/Get Motivated, (2016). Reddit. Retrieved from URL: https://www.reddit.com/r/GetMotivated/comments/4gadww/Text_eric_thomas_resiliency_motivational_speech

Schrage, Michael (2013) *Harvard Business Review*. Retrieved from URL: https://hbr.org/2013/11/is-it-ok-to-yell-at-your-employees

Simon Sinek (2017), *Start With Why*, Retrieved from URL: https://startwithwhy.com/find-your-why

Smith, Jacquelyn, (2013), *Forbes*. Retrieved from URL: https://www.forbes.com/sites/jacquelynsmith/2013/04/18/8-ways-to-achieve-better-work-life-balance/#601efb6caba4

Thompsen, Brian; Roosevelt, Theodore, (2015) *The Man in the Arena: Selected Writings of Theodore Roosevelt: A Reader*. Retrieved from URL: https://www.brainpickings.org/2018/04/30/theodore-roosevelt-arena-cynicism-critic

Toastmasters International (2018), *How To Build A Toastmasters Club Guide*, Rancho Santa Margarita, CA, Toastmasters International

Volunteer Resource Center, (2018) Retrieved from URL: http://www.idealist.org/info/Volunteer/Rights

Vitelli, Romeo, Ph.D. (2013) *Psychology Today, Media Spotlight,* Retrieved from URL: https://www.psychologytoday.com/ca/blog/media-spotlight/201307/can-volunteering-help-you-live-longer

Warrell, Margie, (2013) *Forbes.* Retrieved from URL: https://www.forbes.com/sites/margiewarrell/2013/10/30/Know-your-why-4-questions-to-tap-the-power-of-purpose/#7b8a510c73ad

Williamson, Marianne, (1992), *"A Return to Love: Reflections on the Principles of "A Course in Miracles"* New York, NY, Harper Collins

Wolf Leslie, (2010) *CA Digital Library.* Retrieved from URL: https://www.cdlib.org/cdlinfo/2010/09/15/what-gets-measured-gets-done-key-performance-indicators

FIGURE LIST

ACKNOWLEDGMENTS

We are spiritually blessed to be encouraged and supported by family and friends. First and foremost, thanks to God, who makes all things possible and for paving the way through this incredible journey; and to all those with whom we have crossed paths.

Thank you Shirley (Kitchen), my friend and wife of 27 fun years, for being my inspiration to get this book published; and to our sons, Davidlee and Christopher, who inspire me daily through their ambitions to pursue their own dreams.

Thank you Denise (Lattimore), Lil Marilyn, Danielle and Marquis for reminding us to continue to follow our dreams; and to Kim and Dr. Kay for your inspiring feedback.

Thanks to our Saturday mastermind group; Denicio, Ryan, Sylvester, and Prince, for sacrificing your mornings to hold each other accountable to our goals; and to my brother Paul, for your inspiration to be a great coach and volunteer leader.

Special thanks to Sam and Didi; and Carol and Tom, for your "voluntold" support and to Joan, Carlos, Jessica, Brian, Joyce, and Cho'nee for the wonderful years of serving together in leadership, which contributed to making this book possible.

A big thank you to our colleagues of the Lakewood Toastmasters 1497, The Officers' Club of District One and Edison Power Lines for being part of our leadership journey; to our friends of the Rough Writers Club, for fostering the inspiration to become an author; to Walt for your inspiration and suggestions and to Beth for your book on simplifying the publishing process.

CONTRIBUTORS

Thank you to the following people for contributing your words of wisdoms to this book.

Lydia Boyd – Distinguished Toastmaster and Past International Director, for inspiring us to be leaders and constantly reminding us not to "let the opinion of others become our reality."

Rona Lewis - CEO of PlayMore Corporate Wellbeing, for your relevant input and positive energy in helping others succeed.

ABOUT THE AUTHORS

David Kitchen, MBA, is the founder of "Training Dynamics Network" and a 4-time Distinguished Toastmaster in Toastmasters International. An author, professional speaker, trainer and leadership coach, David possesses executive management and volunteer leadership skills spanning across 30 years. His leadership programs for adults and youth have been acclaimed by fortune 500 companies, school districts, non-profit organizations and workforce agencies. His volunteer leadership experience includes serving in Toastmasters International, Explorer Scouts, Catholic Youth Organization, Paramount Junior Athletes Association, Boy Scouts of America and Tavis Smiley Groups. Visit his website at www.trainingdynamics.org.

Rev. Michael Bernard Lattimore, MA, CISSP is the founder of "Success Support Team" and a Distinguished Toastmaster in Toastmasters International. A Cyber Awareness Evangelist and a volunteer/board member for the "FreedomtoChoose" Prison Project, Michael is a professional speaker and cybersecurity subject matter expert. His volunteer leadership experience includes serving in Toastmasters International, Ahiah Center for Spiritual Living, Agape International Spiritual Center and the Boy Scouts of America. Michael's story is featured in "Mission Possible" alongside such notables as Brian Tracy, Bruce Jenner and Jack Canfield.

TRAINING DYNAMICS NETWORK
Training Tomorrow's Leaders Today!

TDN delivers comprehensive training that employs "real-world" solutions. Seminars are tailored to meet the needs of individuals and organizations large or small. Explore inspirational and technical topics proven to effect positive change and organizational success. All training is experiential using relevant techniques that sustains and reinforces positive results.

TEAM LEADERSHIP WORKSHOPS

- Team Collaboration
- Communications
- Strategic Planning

YOUTH LEADERSHIP WORKSHOPS

- Intro to Youth Leadership
- Advanced Youth Leadership
- Cyber Youth Leadership
- Entrepreneurial Leadership

CYBER LEADERSHIP WORKSHOPS

- Social Media Awareness
- Data Privacy Management
- Cyber Leadership

Reserve Your Workshop Today

Visit our Website: www.trainingdynamics.org
Phone : (562) 548-2284 or Email: info@trainingdynamics.org

ML

MARILEE Publishing